# On Aging

# *On Aging*

## REVOLT AND RESIGNATION

## Jean Améry

TRANSLATED BY JOHN D. BARLOW

*Indiana
University
Press*

BLOOMINGTON AND INDIANAPOLIS

Originally published as *Über das Altern. Revolte und Resignation.*
© 1968 Ernst Klett Verlag für Wissen und Bildung GmbH, Stuttgart

English translation © 1994 by John D. Barlow

The paper used in this publication meets the minimum requirements of
American National Standard for Information Sciences—Permanence of
Paper for Printed Library Materials, ANSI Z39.48-1984.

♾ ™

MANUFACTURED IN THE UNITED STATES OF AMERICA

**Library of Congress Cataloging-in-Publication Data**

Améry, Jean.
  [Über das Altern.   English]
  On aging  :   revolt and resignation / Jean Améry ; translated by
John D. Barlow.
      p.  cm.
  Includes bibliographical references.
  ISBN 0-253-30675-2 (cloth)
  1. Old age—Psychological aspects.   2. Aging—Psychological
aspects.   I. Title.
BF724.8.A4813   1994
155.67—dc20                                                    93-41804
  1  2  3  4  5  99  98  97  96  95  94

J'avais vécu comme un

peintre montant un chemin qui surplombe

un lac dont un rideau de rochers et d'arbres lui cache la

vue. Par une brèche il l'aperçoit, il l'a tout entier devant

lui, il prend ses pinceaux. Mais déjà vient la nuit où l'on

ne peut plus peindre et sur laquelle le jour ne

se relèvera plus!

—Proust, *Le Temps retrouvé*


I had lived like a painter

climbing a road overhanging a lake, a view

of which is hidden from him by a curtain of rocks and

trees. Through a gap he catches a glimpse of the lake, with

its whole expanse before him, and he takes up his brushes.

But already night is coming, the night in which he will

not be able to paint anymore and upon which

no day will follow.

—Proust, *Time Regained*

# Contents

# TRANSLATOR'S PREFACE

In making this translation I have been mindful of the fact that, beginning with *At the Mind's Limits*, all seven of Améry's self-contained books came into being originally as radio talks. Each essay or chapter in each one of them is about twenty-five pages long, basically what Améry could read over the radio in just under an hour. They have an intimate, conversational style that might not be present in writings never intended to be read aloud. Anyone who has heard Améry read over the radio or heard recordings of his readings knows the particularly melancholy and reflective precision of his voice and the hold it can have on the listener. In translating, I have tried to retain this tone as much as possible, even in those occasional passages that seem less convincing, or dated, or more dependent on stereotypical examples.

Even though it is Améry's practice in German to use generic singulars, I have tried to use them only occasionally, partly to avoid the implied gender preference, but also because I find frequent uses of generic singulars and nominal adjectives clumsy, even pompous, in English. Furthermore, to say "aging persons are likely . . ." sounds less sweeping than "the aged person is likely. . . ." I hope readers do not feel this to be an unnecessary violation of Améry's intentions.

I would like to thank three persons in particular for their assistance in this project: John Gallman, Director of the Indiana University Press and editor of this publication, for his assistance and encouragement and for being such a superb editor and university press director; Norma Drake, for clerical assistance; and especially Pat Barlow, for many forms of help and advice.

## TRANSLATOR'S INTRODUCTION

Giacomo Leopardi, who suffered from numerous physical ailments before his life ended at the early age of thirty-eight, still wrote in his *Pensieri* that old age was the greatest evil, far worse than death. To Leopardi, old age stripped human beings of their pleasures, but left them their appetites and brought them every kind of sorrow. He was perplexed that anyone would fear death and want old age. In what was one of his last poems, he wrote how the gods, thinking that the human condition would be too blessed and full of joy if youth could last and that an early death would be too mild, decided to introduce "a stronger doom than terrible death itself":

> And so the eternal ones
> Invented the worst evil known, that fit
> Creation of unaging souls—old age:
> The state in which desire
> Remains intact, our hopes become extinct,
> The sources of our joy run dry, our pains
> Increase, and good comes not again to us.[1]

This is not a very happy or consoling view of old age, and it is made even more dismal by the fact that its author, while never experiencing old age chronologically, could tell from the experience of his youth, wracked with pains and miseries similar to those of old age, what it might be like. Yet most social, psychological, and religious programs of consolation try to overcome this view of old age. It is too hopeless and gloomy. Furthermore, in societies where old age is becoming more and more the norm rather than an exception, it is necessary to resist the debilitating effects of a propensity to depression and sorrow that could afflict the largest proportion of the population. Nonetheless, Leopardi's view is not much different from that presented by Jean Améry in the pages that follow, except that Améry wrote his book when he was fifty-five. He was not suffering from a debilitating disease, and he had survived the worst social nightmare imaginable: torture, deportation, and internment in Auschwitz. It is possible that his Auschwitz experience made him exceptionally susceptible to even the slightest indications of the deciduousness of aging. He wrote, after all, that he believed "that in Auschwitz we did not become better, more human, more humane, and more mature ethically. You do not observe dehumanized man committing his deeds and misdeeds without having all your notions of inherent human dignity placed in doubt. We emerged from the camp stripped, robbed, emptied out, disoriented. . . ."[2] It is also plausible that, in spite of surviving the Holocaust, he retained scars that left him especially impatient with the onset of the inconveniences experienced by human beings in their fifties. Furthermore, as Améry states in the pages that follow, he found the *terror* of his experiences at Auschwitz to be qualitatively different and, incredible to say, less filled with internal *horror* and *anguish* than the experience of aging. To this can be added a fascination with death, perhaps best acknowledged in an essay written in 1973 in which Améry contrasts Elias Canetti's remark, "I *hate* death," with his own "fearful longing" for death and his "having little desire to live long."[3]

In any case, Améry intentionally wrote the essays of *On Aging* to disturb his listeners (they were broadcast over the radio before being published in book form) and readers. His aim was to mince no words about the unpleasantness of the experience of growing old and to demonstrate that existentially one can never know what aging is like until one experiences it. Rather than trying to say what aging could or should be in a more humane society and a more understanding world, Améry wanted to describe what it is. *On Aging* is a most honest book, intentionally eschewing an attempt to make readers feel better. In spite of its starkness, however, it may provide a way of coping with old age based on a recognition of what is coming and being prepared for its arrival.

Jean Améry's life began in Vienna, where he was born in 1911 as Hanns Mayer. His first piece of writing was published in 1928. At the university, he studied philosophy and continued with his aspiring literary efforts, completing a novel, *Die Schiffbrüchigen* (The ship-wrecked), which he sent to Thomas Mann and Robert Musil. The latter said that it was "gifted," but Améry was never able to publish it. When the Nazis came to power in Austria in 1938, Améry fled Vienna, knowing that, since his father was a Jew, he would be persecuted if he stayed. He moved to Belgium, joined the resistance there, was caught distributing leaflets, and eventually, after being tortured and having his identity discovered, was sent to Auschwitz.

He survived the brutality of the Holocaust and returned to Belgium after the war, changing his first name to its French equivalent and rearranging the letters of his last name to become Jean Améry. He made his home in Brussels and became a journalist, writing in German mostly for Swiss publications. But he never thought of this journalistic activity as anything more than writing on consignment. He actually published six books of journalism about jazz, famous contemporaries, including Winston Churchill, and various newsworthy matters. One of the books, published in the early sixties, was about Gerhart Hauptmann, the quintessential model of the opportunistic German writer under both the Nazis and the Marxists.

Throughout this period, Améry felt that he was a failure as a writer. Looking back, he wrote shortly before his death, "My identity as a writer, which I had been seeking since my sixteenth year, when my first manuscript was printed in Vienna, had vanished. I accustomed myself to the situation of a failure or a 'raté.'"[4] All of this changed with the publication in 1966 of *Jenseits von Schuld und Sühne* (*At the Mind's Limits*), a series of essays about his experiences in Auschwitz.[5] As he put it later, "I had escaped the drudgery of writing articles in 1966. I could contemplate writing about the things that were weighing on my soul."[6] He went on to write six more books like *At the Mind's Limits* as well as numerous essays on various subjects, some of which have been gathered together in several book-length collections.

The things that Améry describes as "weighing on my soul" all turn around the frail mortality of human life: aging, suicide, torture, exile, failure, deceived love. Death haunts them all. His interest is to discuss human mortality from the inside, as it were, without calling on moral indignation, social science, or psychological analysis. Thus the chapter on being tortured in *At the Mind's Limits*, establishing the absoluteness of the experience and its permanent impact on the constitution of one who has been tortured. In a book about the fictitious character Charles Bovary, husband of Madame Bovary in Flaubert's novel, Améry tries to get inside the character, treating him as a real human being who had suffered the loss of love and had been duped by the one he loved, in order to defend him against attitudes that mock his simple-mindedness, his trust, that make fun of him because of his spouse's behavior, even to defend him against the author who invented him.[7]

The most controversial of these books was his discourse on suicide, *Hand an sich legen* (literally: "To lay hand on oneself"),[8] published in 1976, two years before Améry took his own life. In this book, he presents a sympathetic view of suicide, using the German word *Freitod* (voluntary death), instead of the more common *Selbstmord* (self-murder), because the former is not judgmental but merely descriptive. In addition to the melancholy contemplation of suicide as a potentially positive action in some circumstances, *Hand an sich legen* offers a probing delineation of Améry's basic concern about what it is and feels like to be within oneself a failure, or a fundamentally unhappy person, without making the political claim of being a victim. Starting from Wittgenstein's aphorism "The world of the happy person is a different world from that of the unhappy person," which serves as an epigraph for the book, Améry seeks to demonstrate that the kinds of experiences that drive one to suicide cannot be understood from outside the individual experiencing them, that the feelings of well-being of those who are not suicidal make them ultimately indisposed to understand the suicidal and their state of mind. As he wrote in a letter, "It is to be a book that entirely presents voluntary death from within so that the author completely enters the closed world of the suicide. Therefore: nothing sociological, nothing psychological in the narrow sense."[9] These reflections are pertinent to considering *On Aging*, to which Améry thought *Hand an sich legen* should be a companion. Just as the suicidal state is one that resists understanding by those who are nonsuicidal, so the terminal state of aging cannot be fully appreciated until one is already aging oneself.

*On Aging: Revolt and Resignation*, published in 1968, was the first of Améry's books after *At the Mind's Limits*. It was also the first he published with the publishing firm of Klett in Stuttgart (later Klett-Cotta), which would publish all subsequent books of his as well as reissue the German text of *At the Mind's Limits*.

When *On Aging* was published, Améry was becoming astonished at—and gratified by—his sudden success in his late fifties.

Each of the essays of *On Aging* covers a particular complex of issues about the experience of growing old. As Monique Boussart points out,[10] an aspect of each is essentially a dialogue with French intellectuals. In the first, it is Marcel Proust, who not only provides much of the reflective commentary with his series of novels *In Search of Lost Time*, especially the last, *Time Regained*, but who also appears in Améry's discussion. The subject here is time, lived time as opposed to calendar and clock time or the time of physics, the way time passes, and the way aging makes the elderly progressively perceive time as the essence of their existence.

The last pages of Simone de Beauvoir's *Force of Circumstance* provide the underpinnings of the next essay, a meditation on the ways the aging are alienated from themselves. The body becomes a burden they carry around with them, even as they come to know it better and to identify with it more. There are, in fact, a number of similarities between de Beauvoir's *Old Age*, first published shortly after *On Aging*, and Améry's reflections, although it seems that each book was written independently of the other.

The third essay deals with social aging, the condition of realizing that it is no longer possible to live according to one's potential or possibilities, but that one must live in sober recognition that one is what one is, or else fall back on a pretense of normality, eternal youth, or an idyll of serenity and satisfaction—or opt for being a crank. This essay draws on Jean-Paul Sartre and André Gorz, as well as the novel *La Quarantaine* by Jean-Louis Curtis. It naturally leads into the fourth essay, on cultural aging, where Améry again calls on Sartre, whom he has written about in other essays and who, along with Simone de Beauvoir, had a strong influence on him immediately after the Second World War.

In cultural aging, the loss of the ability to understand new developments in the arts and in a changing society's values and the feeling of becoming useless and out of touch with the world become everyday aspects of one's existence. The fifth and last essay, on the nearness of death and its effect on the lives of the aging, for whom death and dying are companions, shows the impact of Améry's reading of Vladimir Jankélévitch's *La Mort*, published in 1966. The novel *Les Thibaut* (The Thibauts) by Roger Martin du Gard, describing the death of the old father of the Thibaut family, demonstrates the utter misery of many endings of life. Améry argues that everyone makes a compromise with death in old age, that physical condition in which we feel the death that is in us. It is a compromise that affects our behavior and influences our demeanor. Améry's intention becomes most clear in this essay: to disturb easy and cheap compromises and to urge his readers to their own individual acts of defiance and acceptance.

In addition to French backgrounds, such as those cited above, Améry also calls into play his readings in German literature and thought, especially Thomas Mann, whose meditations on death and disease in *The Magic Mountain* are frequently cited, and the physician Herbert Plügge, whose phenomenological studies of disease and the body Améry has written about elsewhere as well. Améry prefers literary and cultural references for evidence in supporting his views because he does not want to be systematic and because he approaches aging in terms of experience. When he turns to scholars, it is to philosophers like Jankélévitch and Sartre or to practitioners like Plügge who try to describe the way humans feel the experience of aging, even if they often do so in abstract terms that are foreign to Améry, rather than to those who have done studies, made surveys, or otherwise observed from outside. His use of their insights is based on an unusual alliance of French existentialism and Viennese positivism, an alliance that is evident in his analytic approach to many of the culturally accepted ideas and metaphors about old age and death in *On Aging*.

What the reader finds here is a desire to describe old age as it is, in terms of how it is felt and sensed rather than in medical and psychological terms, without consolation and without external support mechanisms: a condition in which human beings tend toward ceasing to be, toward being nothing, toward the negative, being "unable to perform much physical work, uncoordinated, unfit for this and that, unteachable, unfruitful, unwelcome, unhealthy, un-young," as Améry describes it. The only way to deal with this condition is for the aging to cast themselves in an attitude of simultaneous revolt and resignation. Resigned to the inevitability of aging and all its concomitant discomforts, frustrations, and losses, they can save themselves from embarrassment, stress, and the wasted effort of trying to be something they are not by revolting against this condition and refusing to play the social and psychological games: the little jokes and passive sentimentalities, benign community activities, and social service outings that define the old as helpless victims. Implied in Améry's book is the idea that consolation is a form of victimization. He does not want to make people feel better. He wants to "disturb the balance, expose the compromise, destroy the genre painting, contaminate the consolation," as he writes at the end of the book.

Améry, well aware of the contradictory nature of his prescription, refuses to back off from it because of the absurd nature of aging itself. It is a terminal experience, from which there is no recovery. Indeed, Améry calls it a disease, a virus we carry with us from birth. In this, his essays are often reminiscent of the *memento mori* of medieval writers and their emphasis on the necessity of death, only without their theological underpinnings and purpose and with a different motive. He is not trying to convert or teach morality. The key to Améry's book is his determination to look at the phenomenon of aging without blinking, to assess it without sentimentalizing, consoling, or mincing words about the horrible nature of what he sees. It is similar to the stance he took in his autobiographical writings, in his attempt to imagine what it would be like to be Charles Bovary, in his analysis of suicide, and in his meditations on the fate of intellectuals in Auschwitz. Consolation could come, he wrote in *At the Mind's Limits*, if one had a religious faith or an ideological conviction about the inevitability of history in which one's fate could be seen as ultimately redeeming, no matter what the extent of personal suffering. Améry had neither faith nor conviction. In *On Aging*, he notes the role of religious belief and sentiment in preparing for death and in thinking about it, especially in such "metaphorically empty" phrases as "Rest in peace." To Améry, attempts to console and cheer up, to ameliorate old age and death in comfortable formulas, are all part of a "vile dupery" that his book, in a very personal way, aims to expose.

With *On Aging*, Améry was venturing into a merciless reflection on his own condition, an analysis determined to be as much without compromise as possible. It is not surprising that it led eventually to his study of suicide. Moreover, he could not avoid a feeling of superfluousness and irrelevance, as he wrote in one of his last letters barely a week before his suicide, and he even reflected that it may have been "something like an error of fate that in 1945, when I was still relatively young, I did not decide to become a French writer."[11] *When he was still relatively young*: with this kind of regret, about which he could do nothing, the horror of aging was triumphing over him. Améry's suicide, his voluntary death, seems to have been the only road he thought was left to him.

# PREFACE TO THE FOURTH EDITION

In the decade that has passed since I recorded this experiment I could have learned much more about aging. Not without pleasure do I remember the strong criticism when my book appeared, especially that of a gentleman definitely getting on in years who reproached me something like this: what, so he thought, could this "young" person of 55 years, J.A., understand about aging and age? What does he think he's doing?

As I read the text again, I have to say to my own deep regret that the cheerful old man is wrong—and I'm right, alas! I had understood my subject. If I have learned anything in the last ten years, it has lead me instead to accentuate what I said at that time rather than to modify it. Everything has been a trace worse than I had foreseen: physical aging, cultural aging, the daily approach, sensed as a burden, of the dark journeyman who runs along at my side and urgently calls to me as to Raimund's Valentin with the uncannily intimate phrase, "Come, little friend. . . ."[1]

Today as much as yesterday I think that society has to undertake everything to relieve old and aging persons of their unpleasant destiny. And at the same time I stick to my position that all high-minded and reverential efforts in this direction, though indeed capable of being somewhat soothing—thus also being harmless analgesics—are still not capable of changing or improving *anything fundamental* about the tragic hardship of aging.

At one single point I will make a revision, at the very point where I wrote that bad phrase, the "fool's story of a voluntary death." *Here* new insights and learnings have forced me into another direction, have given my reflections an extension that I could not have imagined at that time. Thus, I felt myself bound to write my book on suicide, *By One's Own Hand—A Discourse on Voluntary Death*, which, in a certain sense, can be considered a continuation of the work before us.

Brussels, Spring 1977                                    Jean Améry

## PREFACE TO THE FIRST EDITION

Compelled by nothing more than an inclination to be contemplative, and perhaps to practice being so, I submit here experimental essays about the aging of human beings. Experimental—not in the sense of a scientific experiment, but in that of looking for something whose undiscoverable nature was obvious to analytic reason from the start. These meditations about my subject have nothing to do with geriatrics. They deal with *aging* human beings in relation to time, to their own bodies, to society, to civilization, ultimately to death. Readers who expect remarks of a positive scientific nature on the subject, the kind of knowledge that could assist them in preparing their lives for a particular condition—that of aging—will be disappointed by this book: I cannot aspire to anything like that.

In an era when intelligence is turning away not only from what is immediately given by consciousness but from *the human being* in general—in whose place systems and codes appear as the subject of inquiry—I have kept entirely to what has been lived: *le vécu*. In making this effort to record as faithfully as possible the developments in which the aging person is ensnared, I used essentially a method of introspection; added to that was a striving for observation and empathy. But any hope for scientific method, even logical stringency, had to be abandoned.

If, on the one hand, the subjective character of such notes has been self-evident to me from the beginning, I have still tried, on the other hand, to direct the process toward observations that are more than subjective. I have constantly tried to mirror from every visual angle the ideas I've formed by means of a thought process that constantly contests and corrects itself, one that never shies away from contradiction—all of this, it is true, while consciously deviating from the goals of objectivity or intersubjectivity. I was only carried along by the uncertain hope that I might succeed in illuminating a few fundamental facts, valid for the typical human being of our civilization. Out of that came a wager: decisions about whether I was making sense or not, about the value of my work or the lack of it, are left entirely to my readers, since that third authority that makes a judgment of truth could not be invoked.

In addressing my readers, I am requesting them to join with me in something that was revealed to me only while I was writing it down. Specifically, as I felt my way forward, step by step, I had to give up the hopes always evoked by the aging; I had to invalidate consolation. Whatever there is in consolation that is recommended to the aging—how to come to terms with one's decline and fall, even if possible to be able to gain assets from it, nobility of resignation, evening wisdom, late tranquility—it all stood before me as a vile dupery, against which I had to charge myself to protest with every line. Thus, even though I neither planned nor even surmised in advance how they would turn out, my experiments, in quality more like searches, went from being an analysis to being an act of rebellion, whose contradictory premise was the total acceptance of inescapable and scandalous things. I can only wait and see if the readers I am addressing answer me, if they accompany me on my way through these contradictions.

Even if I dispense with every allegedly scientific instrument and base my point of view entirely on myself and the uncertain ground of my questioning, it is still only too obvious that I have been subject to numerous influences. Readers can recognize them as easily as they can my quotations, occasionally structured into the text and as such not expressly indicated.

But there are three authors from whom I have learned much and whom I have to introduce explicitly since they are possibly not sufficiently well known: the Sorbonne professor Vladimir Jankélévitch, the German physician and phenomenologist Herbert Plügge, the French publicist André Gorz.[1]

No author can bring out the results of his restless hours without being anxious. When one writes about the most personal things in the hope that, here and there, despite every self-restriction, they could be transformed into something universally binding, the dread is even greater. Books do not only have their own destiny: they can also be a destiny.

Brussels, Summer 1968                                   Jean Améry

*On Aging*

# Existence and the Passage of Time

The aging human being—the aging woman, the aging man—we will frequently meet such persons here, presenting themselves to us in many variants, in many different kinds of dress. At one point, we will recognize an aging person as a figure well known to us from a work of literature; in another place she will be a pure abstraction drawn from the imagination; finally, he will be revealed in his contours as the author of this series of essays. The actual number of years will be just as indefinite as the person who is aging, just as it is in reality and in the way we use language. We will see the aging when they are only around forty, because in certain circumstances the process we are going to try to describe announces itself early on. In other examples, they will enter as human beings in their sixth decade, each therefore actually becoming a senex, according to a vague statistical objectivity. Here, where we are dealing with *existence and the passage of time*, let's introduce one of them as a man scarcely fifty years old, whose early death would certainly justify that at this age he already felt he was an aging person, therefore requiring us also to accept him as such. —We meet him as he appears once again at a morning reception for the first time after many years. A long time ago, he had withdrawn from this vanity fair in which he had once played a significant part. He is dressed in a frock coat, very upright, still in good posture even if his chest and belly appear arched forward in a not quite natural and somewhat uncanny way. His thick black hair, lying down the nape of his neck, and his mustache are still their natural color, but his pale face above his high collar is as rigid as wax, like a mask, and his orientally melancholy eyes are without luster, resting in the shadow of deep, bluish rings.

We'll call this aging man by the cipher "A.," just as we'll designate all those of his comrades in destiny whom from time to time we intend to introduce to our considerations. A.: both the most mathematical and abstract specification imaginable and one that leaves to my readers the most extensive free space to think imaginatively and concretely. This time, however, let's call this, our first A., by the name the world gave him: the *narrateur* or, as an exception that is still more precise, by his civil name, strangely pronounced "Pruh" in his home département Loir-et-Cher, the person we know as Proust—*Marcel Proust*.

Hat in hand, A. —Marcel Proust—enters the home of his hosts and discovers while doing so that the servants of the house recognize him again in spite of years of absence. There comes father Proust, these people say—and since he has no son, he knows that "father" can only relate to his age. If the servants knew the situation better and could express themselves more clearly, they would say that the scarcely fifty-year-old man, in spite of his unbleached hair and his standing there so straight and tall, looks, in a way that is hard to define, older than his years, especially because in his unmoving yellow-white face rigor mortis is already anticipated. —The *narrateur* sees people again who, if the inspection of his eyes were not deceptive, are worse off than he himself is. Who is the fairy-tale king with the cotton beard, dragging himself along as though his shoes had leaden soles? The Prince de Guermantes; it—an "it" about which we will speak long and much—had happened to him. And who's the old man, whose white beard no longer looks like an actor's prop on an amateur stage but like the beard of a beggar? Monsieur d'Argencourt, no doubt, the *narrateur's* intimate enemy of some time ago. The Baron de Charlus, once haughty and superb, has become a tragic drawing-room Lear, diligently removing his hat to people who in his better days were not even worthy of his raised eyebrow. Bloch, the companion of earlier times, is now called Jacques du Rozier and wears a formidable monocle to relieve his aged face of the task of showing any kind of expression. —The visitor comes upon human beings whose eyelids have the sealed rigidity of those about to make their exit, whose constantly murmuring lips seem to be uttering the prayers of those already singled out for death.[1] Sclerosis has thoroughly restructured others and made them into stone-like Egyptian gods. The *narrateur* even finds some who seem hardly changed as long as they are observed from a distance; seen up close in conversation, however, their apparently still-smooth skin reveals such swellings to the observer, such tiny nodules and reddish-blue capillary vessels that they arouse even more violent aversion and deeper horror than those whose age announces itself without concealment in their colorless hair, crooked backs, and dragging legs. The guest recognizes most of them again, he has seen them, spoken with them a long time ago at some *dîner en ville*, and through their sclerosis and dehydration, he can decode the features of the past. But it also happens that someone addresses him, whose face, voice, and figure leave him helpless. A fat lady greets him with her "*bonjour.*" A. looks at her, querulous, and begs her pardon: it is Gilberte, whom he had loved in Combray as a boy and on the Champs Elysées. —But what has really happened to these people that Proust's *narrateur* has found again at this reception of the Prince de Guermantes? Not much. Everything. *Time has passed.*

Time has passed, flowed by, rolled on, blown away, and we pass with it—what am I saying? —like smoke in a strong wind. We ask ourselves what time might actually be, about which we say that everything glides and runs by with it—ask ourselves with a tenacious naïveté that borders on total ridiculousness, and then are taught by those thinkers who are so adroit in logical play that the question, when asked in such a banal form, is deceptive. —A few exploratory experiments with the idea of time throw us into total confusion: just exactly what that very old and clever bird-headed Englishman says, following Zeno, in an amusing paradox. Does the past exist? No, because it is already gone. Does the future exist? No, because it has not yet come. Then is there only the present? Of course. But isn't it so that this present contains no stretch of time? It is so. Then there is no such thing as time at all. Correct: it doesn't exist. Russell's paradox can be solved. Answers exist to many questions about time, and sufficiently sharp and well-trained thinkers have tried to find them. But what they've come away with has little to do with our concerns.

In thinking about time, when we are not talking about the time of physicists, for whom it is something quite different than it is for us, but about *our* time, which is always *only* ours, our lived time, our *temps vécu*—in such thinking, we step forward between two dangerous zones, both of which are equally fatal. On the one hand, we are threatened by dull ruminations and dilettantish brooding. On the other, we have the technical language of the specialist in the discipline of philosophy, which, in sounding learned, strives to prove its own significance more than the value of its knowledge. And yet, we have to try to press on, because it is time, lived time, or, if you will, subjective time, which is our most urgent problem. Problem? Once again a word from the newspaper, smelling offensively of printer's ink. Time is our arch enemy and our most intimate friend, our only totally exclusive possession and, as we never seem to realize, our pain and our hope. It is difficult to speak of it. Down from the magic mountain we hear: can time be narrated, this time itself, as such, in and for itself? Definitely not; that would be a foolish enterprise. A story that proceeded to tell that time flowed, it ran on, time streamed along, and on and on—no one could sensibly call that a story. —It would not only not be a story, as that famous magician, Thomas Mann, thought, but it would also have nothing more to do with time than the fact that it would take a little time, even if only just a little. Flowing away, running on, streaming along, time does not do these things; such things take place in space, experienced visibly or at least as a consequence of what is seen. When we talk of time, we use figures of speech from the world of space, "spatiomorphic metaphors," as one might say to sound scholarly. Time is hardly narratable. We say "hardly" and not *un*narratable. Otherwise we would have to remain silent instead of still eventually saying something, as we struggle to do, in the space between the two danger zones. Figures of speech may be useful as long as their figurative nature is constantly acknowledged. And we can employ our considerations, even those without epistemological value, when we succeed in describing things in which others can discover themselves again.

For a long time A. had been concerned with the tormenting questions of aging, existence, and the passage of time. Now he was visiting one of his friends, a famous physicist, hoping the latter would be able to give him some advice in making sense of these impenetrable things. This man of science immediately took over the conversation, and things quickly became lofty and high-spirited. Time? A problem of physics. Once we had the classical physics of Newton in which time was not yet really time. That is, time, since it was only a matter of the movement of bodies in space, could be reversed. The position of the moon, for instance, was just as easy to predict in advance for the year 2500, on the basis of accepted data, as it was in reverse for the year 1600. Then, with modern physics, came the time of thermodynamics, irreversible time, time tied to the concept of entropy, a measurement for the improbability of the order of molecules resulting by chance, a tendency that leads to a generally increasing disorder, the extreme case of which is so-called heat death. Popularly and briefly formulated: thermodynamic time is not reversible because it tends toward the decay of all being. Nonetheless, the physicist would concede that one could also speak of a "biological" time which, reversed, would cause the construction and not the dissolution of structures. However, biological time would not concern him, at least not until statements about it can be translated in their entirety into a mathematical-physical language.

None of this was very "clear" to our troubled A., but it was, even in a slightly questionable way, something he could latently deal with, somewhat intuitively, so that he partly knew what his friend was talking about. For him, however, rather than for the professor, it was not a question of movements of bodies in space, nor of heat death, for which for God's sake there was still plenty of time, nor even a question of time deduced from the facts of evolution. He was speaking of years passing away, of memories that suddenly appeared and deceptively suspended time, of the weight of death sensed in the plain results of time. With conceptual impatience, the man of positive knowledge indicated with a nodding gesture that he was disinclined to proceed in this vein. Since he was not just a brainy and rigid specialist, however, but a culturally circumspect human being, philosophically well read, with the intellect of a generalist, even familiar with that other cultivated person whom we met at the Guermantes', he said, "I know, *durée vécue*, Bergson, Minkowski, irrationalism, phenomenological mental games, I'm right in the picture. But I ask you, what is all that to me, I who deal with space and time in my equations, space and time insofar as they are of course definable and capable of being wrapped up in formulae?" What was it in fact to him? A. thanked him and slinked off humbled, brooding in his unclear head as he was wont to do, not even able to forgive himself for having dared to engage such a serious investigator with such undeveloped half-thoughts.

Long after that he happened to meet his friend again. This time the man was discouraged and tired, no longer predisposed at all to sticking arrogantly to the subject. "How time has run away from me," said the scholar. "How long has it been that we have known one another? Twenty years? My God, what plans I once had, what all didn't I want to do that I still haven't done. And what I would still like to finish if only I were granted the time. But too much time has already gone by and I have so little time left." "Oh, miraculous time, oh, to spend time—", this the physicist did not say anymore; A. was thinking thus within, somewhat mechanically; and he parted yet once more from his friend, without consolation, as if he were neither capable of it nor appointed to it. Once again he heard the words of Immanuel Kant, words he had heard so often, words that had been familiar to him since his youth, in which he again and again rediscovered himself and his meditations on time, regardless of the fact that even modern logic and dialectics had already made short shrift of them. Space and time were, in spite of all attempts of modern philosophy to construct a spatiotemporal solidarity, alien to one another. Time is the form of an *inner* sense, that is, the form through which we perceive ourselves and our condition. Wasn't that obvious? At any moment A. could pace off space and find himself within it. The outer sense was the sense of our senses; what took place in space was discussable. But whatever happened with the "inner sense" left little of itself to communicate, and those who dared to go inside themselves to look for its traces and its objects found no reward for their courage and were threatened by an intellectually desolate nothingness. Wherever reality was spatial and words failed, one could still carry out actions that replaced those words. What is blue? That can hardly be explained; but A., when asked about the color blue, could still point to his folder and say, "Here—now—is blue." But how, on the other hand, could he make his feeling for time accessible to another? For that, there was no index finger pointing to anything that could be perceived intersubjectively. One had to wait until others came by themselves to the subject of time and spoke of it. That's what had just happened. Out of his own need and with the same words, spurned as banal equally by science and by the discipline of philosophy—in "idle talk," as it would be called by Martin Heidegger, dressed in a waistless jacket in a ski hut surrounded by a roaring wind—the physicist had spoken of time, because even he was no longer a young man.

The time of which we become aware in aging is not only something we cannot grasp; it is also filled with absurdity, a bitter mockery of every intellectual precision we have aspired to. Some of us expect something good: but the time of good expectations, this "good" time, becomes our enemy, we want to get it behind us as quickly as possible, want to "expel" it or even "kill" it. And something bad threatens others: here the "bad" time becomes our only friend, to whom we hold ourselves like a man condemned to death: he still has five hours till his execution, then two more; finally, when the steps outside can already be heard, it's just a few minutes, seconds, and the poor sinner would like to make this most horrible moment tarry a while because it is so lovely.[2] —Or take a young man with a great deal of time before him, so much that he docsn't want to bother with it; he doesn't need to know anything about it at all. Feeling healthy in his body, he is so sure of himself he doesn't even need the statistics that grant him, the twenty-year-old, fifty more years of life—an unfathomable stretch of time. He is in the process of living on for a vast period of time with the good knowledge and conscience of his twenty years. But tomorrow he will drive his car into a plane-tree and lie dashed to pieces on the *route nationale*. Then he will have *lived falsely* with his plans and vague hopes, because for a life that has come to an end, the end—the early end in this case—is the truth of the beginning and all its stages, and this early end now throws its pale light on all phases of the young life gone by. But even then, when we reach an age that corresponds even halfway to our expectations and our statistically measured time, our time, parceled out and defined with clocks and calendar pages, is still immense, bound-less in the real meaning of the word. Stretches of time or masses of time are relative, not only with regard to intersubjective physical time, which, after all, does not make sense to us, but also with regard to each other. Their relations thereby do not remain the same.

A. has gone through the war, World War II with its service at the front, its wounds, its bombings, its loss of relatives, and its expulsions from the homeland. For him, the mass of time for the years 1939–1945 is opaque and heavy. The ten years preceding the war experience have become just as lifeless, thin, and slight in his memory as the two postwar decades; five years are a longer, weightier time than ten or twenty. But without being noticed, the temporal weights have now become distributed in a new way. Grass has been growing over the entire past, which suddenly appears now to be leveled, no longer having any time value at all. Until—one usually discovers it with a blow—the displacement of the quanta of the past, which has continued to take place under the grass, becomes manifest: then the time of the war is no more tedious than the time after it, and what now appears as a mass of time, like a mountain, is perhaps just a few summer weeks, very far away, that brought with them an already half-forgotten love affair.

We never establish a reasonable relationship with clock and calendar time. Furthermore, we never even get along in *our own* time, which still constitutes our entire ego. We did spend boring and amusing days, at least that's what we say, casually and without embarrassment. However, if we try once again to acclimatize ourselves to those long and short periods of the time of our former days, we discover that something's not right. It was, to be sure, not a very long while at all that we spent in the boredom of monotony, but a frighteningly short one, reviving itself completely shriveled up and null in our memory. Time that was entertaining because it was eventful we recognize as a long time and a great time. The clock ticks regularly. Today I tear off the page of a calendar just as I did yesterday and just as I will do tomorrow when it—an "it" about which we still need to talk—does not interrupt me unexpectedly. Nevertheless, the pace of time does not keep in step. I do it myself, within time and with time, and imagine that I am, if not a brave marcher of this life, at least an orderly one—: until I recognize that at one time I raced breathlessly around, while in another I dragged myself sluggishly along, a lazybones and a malingerer.

So—would we, starting from a different point and by completely different paths, come to the same witty and paradoxical observation that our bird-headed, discerning Englishman came to—that time does not exist? Nonsense! Time is always *within* us, just as space is *around* us. We can no more talk time away than we can our existence, even if it is something that no one completely thinks through. But can't we still take possession of it?

We can. We find time in *aging*—even if we do not, like A. *de chez Guermantes*, entertain the poetic illusion that we have made up for it as *temps retrouvé* in our memory, placed it in suspension, and thereby insinuated ourselves into eternity.

How I've been running, thinks A., and he wipes his brow with his hand. I've been running at a trot through time since the end of the war, and now I'm tired and feel compelled to rest a bit by the side of the road. Yesterday—when the blood and the death were over, I thought a great future was coming toward me. At the time we were blindly running on the Left Bank in total rage toward that future. Saint-Germain-des-Prés, La Rose Rouge, Sartre, from the resistance to the revolution. But time ordered things differently, and out of the wild gallop there grew a regular trot, the latter perhaps more tiring than the former. I arranged myself to fit into a world that I had wanted to be different but which in its way wanted me different and in that very unequal battle carried off the victory. The enticement of a false bourgeois respectability. An apartment, small; a car, small. A bank account, only for the sake of an occasional remittance. But still: apartment, car, and bank account, attained at a tiring trot, and the freedom of the garret, the freedom of one who totally had counted on nothing, is gone—with time and in time. —

How I have been running, A. thinks in exhaustion, and now, whatever happens, I am taking time to catch my breath and to think things over, for the streets are becoming longer and longer and my legs shorter and shorter. My breath is getting heavier, my muscles weaker, my brain more ridiculous. But even with a ridiculous brain, you can still think about existence and the passage of time and the aging process marking your brow, better even than with a highly sharpened intellect, since the latter is always creating order while you, if you really want to keep track of time, are still supposed to give way to disorder.

You've got to make it your intellectual ambition, A. thinks, to try to find out about time. You may be satisfied even if whatever comes out of it is bad as long as it is right, by which "right" won't mean "correct," just "honest." Is that meant to be something like intuitive knowledge? Heavens, no! This kind of bad, but correct, thinking is only for describing one's own way. The rest would be literature or philosophy, and they are good for nothing at all in this matter.

Rigorous reason, a worthwhile instrument of thought and, to be sure, the only one that is qualified to pursue positive knowledge, proves itself to be useless wherever fundamental contradictions exclude the complete justification of something. In keeping track of time, we pass over certain rules of conventionally logical thought. There are no valid regulations even for what we want to express because time, unlike space, is not acquainted with the logic of reality. Past, present, future, the first behind me, the second beside me and with me, the third before me: such are the claims of the way we speak and ordinarily think. That they cannot be correct with regard to the present is the first and most trivial idea that gets in our way, since, as we said already in agreement with Russell, the present does not contain a stretch of time. We've been helping ourselves along with artificial concepts: time cannot be a line from the past that connects by the shortest path a starting point to an end, but is instead a "field of intentionalities." Ordinary language usage, which has not listened to the phenomenologist and has not needed to, since it still mirrors the everyday reality that it all comes down to—ordinary language has known all along that that's more or less the way it is. We talk about a "present" and certainly never mean an ideal point that cannot be extended. Whoever talks about the present unconsciously construes from a class of data a system, a "field," if that's a more appealing expression. In a particular context, I say "now." This "now" contains in itself certain past and future quanta. Depending on how that which is said and done fit together to define it, it can be the moment of a sensual impulse or the instant when I burn my finger with a cigarette, as well as the four weeks of vacation I am now spending by the sea or the current year in which my career takes a new turn. I am in the midst of it in weeks or in a year, but I say "now," I lay out a field of time that includes a future and a past and call it the present. And thus time is not a personal problem for anyone who is living for the world—until, of course, the moment when one realizes, "Alas, where have all my years gone."[3] Only then, when one becomes aware of what has disappeared and gone beyond recall, as A. does, settling down by the wayside, does one understand time as a question directed at oneself.

Attempts to find an answer to this question come to a standstill. Very suddenly neither line nor field are sufficient. The past is there, in the present, and it stays there. But the present and the future lose their character as time. The present is constantly swallowed up by the past, and the future fares no better. But this is always discovered and grasped only by those who are aging, because not much at all is or can be in store for them any more, quite sensibly. One of them starts to say, but with reservation, to a departing friend: "We'll see each other again in a year." He has, he *is*, completely time, because he does not exactly believe any more in the world and what's in store for him.

Those who say that even the young possess and know time, even though they thoughtlessly live for the future dimension, which is also time, such persons have never yet had the experience of feeling for themselves that time is nothing-but-time. This future into which the young tumble like our A. in the days of the Rose Rouge and existentialism is, to be sure, not time at all: it is *world* or, more exactly, it is *space*. The young say of themselves that they have time before them. But what really lies before them is the world, which they absorb and by which they let themselves at the same time be branded. The idea is that the old have life behind them, but this life that is no longer actually lived is nothing but time gathered up, lived, passed away. The less time we think we have before us, since our body and statistics do not hide anything, the more time there is *in* us—and even if the Prince de Guermantes and the Monsieur d'Argencourt had not changed externally, so that A. would have had no effort in recognizing them, they would still be old, old from the time that lies heavily within them. To the young, that which they believe to be time becomes consciously an impatient *expectation* for what is coming to them and is properly due to them after the course of life and death. Time is for them something that obviously moves in space and will enter and step into their life and into them. Characteristically, one is more likely to say of a young person that the *world* is open to him rather than that he has time before him. The old or aging person, however, experiences the future daily as the negation of the spatial and thereby of what is really going on. The future, we are saying, is not time, but it is world and space. Who hasn't already experienced the future in this way for many an hour of everyday life! We wait with impatience for something to happen. The impetuosity of waiting disturbs us. We get up from our seat, walk restlessly back and forth, leave the house in order to make it—a spatial and cosmic occurrence—happen. We even take a car or train if necessary toward this time that is both time and space. But those who have nothing or just a little or only something inessential to expect, who climb down into the past with its deep well,[4] they stay quietly in their place. They sit there sunken into themselves, assume an embryonic position in bed, close their eyes in order to search in themselves, in useless labors of love, for what used to be life, what once was world, was space, but now is only just time. To be old or even just to feel oneself aging means to have time in one's body and in what we call, for short, one's soul. To be young is to throw one's body out into a time that is *no time at all*, but life, world, and space.

Bleakly A. tells himself, It hasn't been so long since I threw myself into the world from the Rive Gauche, only about twenty years. I sense those years as a minor span of time in a way that frightens me to death. The wrinkles in my brow, revealed to me by the mirror, don't concern me; I see through them and, along with them, all the reflections I have ever looked at in those departed two decades. But in another twenty years, I won't be here anymore: how little world I still have before me! Those who believe they have what is called "time" *in front of them*, know that they are truly destined to step out into *space*, to externalize themselves. Those who have life within them, i.e., authentic time, have to be internally satisfied with the deceptive magic of memory.

What is in store for them is death; it will take them completely out of space, their selves and whatever remains of their bodies, it will de-space them, it will take life and the world from them and abduct them from the world and their own space. Thus, as aging persons they are still only time: which they are completely as persons who are time, possess time, and know time.

But doesn't that make life a kind of being-toward-death? Just because time has to make death grow to fruition and because in that process its pure temporality becomes transparent, isn't therefore the real dimension of being human precisely the future as time? It is and it isn't, and in the yes-and-no that serves as an answer to this question the no carries more weight than the yes. To wait for death and therefore be in time—that won't lead anywhere. For when I wait, then there is always something, the arrival and future of which fulfills the time of my waiting. Thus the young man waits, waits for the woman he loves, for the landscape he would like to see, for the work that he is planning as his own. But where death comes into play as the goal of one's expectation, where, for the aging, this death, as the expected, increases its proportion of reality every day and any other reward for waiting comes in comparison to nothing, it is no longer possible to speak of time-in-the-future. For the death that we expect is not a something. It is the denial of every kind of something. To wait for it is not a being-toward-it because it is nothing. Death does not save the future as a dimension of time. On the contrary, through its total negativity, through the complete debacle that cannot be rescinded and that is its meaning (insofar as we can still even speak of meaning, which is only conditionally admissible), death cancels the sense of every kind of reason. It is not the bony man with his scythe and hourglass who "takes us home"—and where would that home be, anyway? It is the result, contradictory in itself, of my being taken out of space in the most literal meaning of the word: my an-nihilation.

In addition, it is not until one is aging that one experiences time as irreversible in its entirety. We speak of the "autumn of life"—charming metaphor! Autumn? After autumn comes a winter, after that once again a spring and then a summer. For the aging, however, the autumn of life is the last autumn and therefore not an autumn at all. The young are never presented with time's irreversibility in its complete inexorability. Autumn, winter, spring, summer, and autumn once again. Many such seasonal changes lie before them. What won't turn up in the early part of this year will come in the next, in the year after next, in any one of the following springs, not objectively enumerated, to be sure, yet in a subjective way genuinely appearing to be innumerable, seasons that will still be preparing world and space for them. Only the aging, who all at once know how to count the autumns and the winters with horrifying exactness, since they still measure the seasons against those that have passed and gone into them, understand the passage of time as an irreversibility—too horrible to complain about, since so much has slipped by and already run past.

Once the aging realize that they are only just time and will soon be removed from space, a number of illusionary comforts appear to them, besides even the greatest and most beguiling illusion of all, religion. A. —Proust—when asthma plagued him and he scribbled away on the *Recherche* in bed in his sealed room, muffled up in wool scarves, thought he could take possession in memory of a more real reality and along with it something like timelessness or even eternity. As a result, a great work of literature came into being. But, when he came to his last breath and he was torn from the world in agony, his achievement was no longer useful to him. Others look into their space to see what it will be like after them: a house where children and their children's children will be active and will work; a tombstone, gray and powerful, will testify for them; their books will be on shelves or their paintings will hang on museum walls. But the house will deteriorate and the grandchildren will be scattered to all the winds, and the books and the pictures will quickly be forgotten. In the Parisian cemetery Père-Lachaise one can see mausoleums, falling apart and neglected, with rats nesting in them. Words are written on them in faded gold: *"Concession à perpétuité"* (plot purchased in perpetuity), as if a bourgeois fortune could at least acquire a pseudo-eternity in space. House and home, book, picture, and tomb, everything will be like the nights of love and pain of the deceased: as good as if they had never existed.

It may be that the passage of time in aging is most intensely felt by a person whose life always seems to be foundering, a *raté* or failure dispossessed of all illusions, just as lack of success, or, better, cosmic failure, opens a person up to ultimate questions. The *raté* A., alone in a café, who has no children and cannot claim to the mirage of fame after death, who will not have his own gravestone erected, and does not even have to make a will, calculates instead that it would be best to sell his own cadaver to the anatomical institute—he knows more fundamentally than others that he is only a bundle of time. He has always possessed only a little bit of space, ever since nothing came of "casting himself into the world." He is accustomed to let himself slide into the well of the past and to look for himself there in time. His neighbor with the big car and many rooms races noisily around until one day a pain in his chest seems to tear him open as if he had been hung on a meat hook and the doctor talks softly to his wife of cardiac infarction; he is taken out of space before he even has the intention of finding the time to think about time. But the aging *raté* has a good idea about where he has come to and, even if he does not really "know" in the sense of having useful insights for his future in space, he still *experiences* it—more than the loud man in the house next door.

One thing that validates what we are presenting here as almost being humanly correct—though not true! —that time and its irreversibility are only fully realized in aging, is the burning and just as hopeless wish of those getting on in years for the *reversal of time*. What has happened should unhappen, what has not happened should take place. A. has regrets. He should have done one thing and let another be, but he has to realize that doing and not doing are no longer rescindable: he cannot bestow to his past life the sense and the value that he would want to give it now, because he no longer recognizes the meaning he would formerly give it and the value it would hold. Instead of waiting for revolution to emerge from *résistance,* maybe he should have worked with great exertion in the years after 1945 on nothing else but developing his language. But now it is too late, the sense of his life, a nonsense when he looks at it exactly, is already gathered up in him as a mass of time. The real has washed over what was once possible, the substance to be dealt with can no longer be molded. He regrets that he has dawdled. Now he has already missed the boat. Wherever he looks he sees on the wall: never again.

Perhaps this regret and this "never again," both of which one can be certain about even without completely and unconditionally believing in them, lie at the basic source of the fear of death. After all, death not only removes us from space but it also destroys the time that has been stacked up inside us. Consequently, not even our regret, which for all its hopelessness still maintains a trace of absurd hope, is able to exist any more. With time, even our longing for its reversal has to disappear. "Let time turn back in its tracks—let us be as we were twenty years ago—let it be last week—let it be yesterday evening!" say King Béranger and Queen Marie.[5] But time does not turn back—*et le roi se meurt*. The more definitively we recognize ourselves as aging persons, the more exactly we experience time in its irreversibility, the more in despair we fight against it, and at the same time and in the same breath the more intimately we belong to it. It is everything that we still are: we can no more give it up than we can give ourselves up, even though we know that we will lose it and ourselves, tomorrow, in the course of the year, in five, in ten years; it really doesn't matter anymore.

We were saying that an aging human being is a bundle of time or a stratified mass of time. That doesn't mean that one can take the bundle apart and put it back together at will, that one can feel through the layers, that one can be the lord of one's time. Psychiatrists teach us that the mentally ill are disoriented in space and time. Whatever kind of space is valid for those suffering from mental illness, it is an attribute of even a healthy person's being in time. The aging, when they plunge down into time, fall, like water from rock to rock, into something uncertain.[6] With relative certainty, they can read the past in the tabulations of physical time, although even that is not always successful. They are not always sure that it was five years ago or four, and they hesitate in giving the exact time when telling the story. Of greater consequence, however, is the fact that the grid the aging use to communicate with others when they itemize periods of time doesn't concern them, that "five-years-ago" feels no different from "fifteen-years-ago," that while the individual layers of time may change their specific gravity for them, such a change has nothing to do with chronology. It is in this sense that those who have discovered their time live completely unhistorically.

For A., who intends to regain time at the home of the Prince de Guermantes, the events he remembers have no chronological order. The face of his mother over his bed, the sound of the iron garden gate shutting when Swann came to visit, an evening with Saint-Loup in Doncières, the taste of the madeleine cookie, and the memory of a dress of the Duchess Oriane, all differentiate themselves through degrees of intensity without gaining any significance for him. Just like the rest of us, A. had lost his way in time. Intervals, days, weeks, years, did not matter to him any more than the time dissipated by the other brothers did to the monk of Heisterbach on his return home to vespers.[7] Because the time that he found again did not have a chronological structure, because it was moreover only *lived* time and as such independent of biographically fixed dates, A. looked for it in the levels of intensity of what had died away. But they were also changing in time and with time. Even before he was taken out of space, he himself stepped out of spaciality and the world given in the present, of which he said that he had seen it previously only through his "deceitful senses." He gave up the world to become time, to become himself: he remembered what was stratified in him as time, because he was too tired to keep wanting to express himself. All he had was the fear of death, because it did not just remove the body from space but also withdrew from this body its *time*. It took from him the time he had lived through, time in which he alone had been able to find that self to which he, living *dans le monde* (in the world), the world understood here as both phenomenal field and "elegant society," had not been granted any right of possession.

A. remembered and reminded *himself*: i.e., he became himself in remembering. What he didn't tell us about in his notes about his actual *recherche du temps perdu*, is that kind of time that even those people sense weighing inside themselves whose memories fade away and who are not inclined, or lack the strength, to try to find themselves. —The aging—not just to speak of the old or even the drowsy and very old—feel the weight of time strata even when they are not fumbling after them in memory. The feeling is constantly present within them—and not only because of the diminishing powers of their bodies or the increasing sufferings these bodies cause them—that they carry *time* inside themselves and therefore do not even need to realize the past in their memory. A time-past is present, even without each memory, as a pure feeling, an immediate and incommunicable quality. In order to symbolize it in language, we have to bring in metaphors from the world of space, if we are to say anything at all about it. The weight of time rests even in someone who can still remember only a few incidents that give it substance. With that it becomes *pure* time, making the "inner sense" present, more authentic to us than the "outer sense," the perceptual form of spaciality.

Space, even *my* space, the possession of which gets me through the spatial form of intuition, is likewise and always the space of others: an intersubjectively understandable phenomenon. There is nothing immediate about it, nor is there any incommensurability between lived space and the measurable space of science. But with my time I am alone, no matter how much I may be required to communicate it. Thus, the feeling of time has a dramatic aspect that is not in the least comparable to that of the feeling of space.

An A. we know well lay tied down for six months in a half-dark solitary cell. He had no space, partly because the cell was tiny and only slightly lit, partly because his bonds kept him from moving. In the long run, he got used to it; he did not lack space once he had accepted the fact of his withdrawal from the world. But his lived time manifested itself with a much greater density. From minute to minute and second to second, it so thoroughly became the past inside him that the supper of soup he had enjoyed an hour earlier was no less distant from him than the childhood experience he had just remembered. He was already half removed from space, and he discovered at that point, once and for all, that lived time in certain circumstances has to compensate for world: the former was entirely his possession and his authenticity, but by the latter he was constantly duped. When we take up the prospect of self-realization, we hope to engrave our seal upon the world. But then it transpires that every die is obliterated by another. A potential will does not lead to becoming an ego, nor to taking possession of the world. It is only a breathless losing of ourselves to foreign powers that are overpowering us.

In the end, A., in his cell in the midst of the many paradoxes and absurdities he bumped into while reflecting on existence in space and time, came to realize the one great fact that all other ambiguities and contradictions hold enclosed in themselves: that by being-in-the-world, by being cast into the world of space, an ego is not yet possible, an ego will only come into being in the struggle against the world and in gentle play with it; that by the time an ego has consolidated itself in one's mind, it is *time* run by, time without world, and this shadowy ego-in-time has the emotional quality of inert mourning and resignation; that eventually neither the ego-in-the-world nor the ego-in-time can be *reality*.

And yet all of us are still real and a part of reality as long as we remain in space and carry time within us. Only when our all-too-strenuous meditations about existence and the passage of time, condemned to futility from the start, have driven us into madness or suicide, are the contradictions finally resolved in the absurdity of lunacy or self-destruction. Therefore, A.'s state of mind in his cell was different from that of some of the comrades with whom he later discussed the nature of time spent in such solitary confinement under a threat of death. Many of them had not given up the hope that comes from the desire to cast themselves into the world. A. looked ahead to his expected end without great fear. Not because he was courageous—he wasn't—but because he had become as tired as the guest of the Guermantes when he left the prince's *matiné* to go to work in his cork-paneled room. All his meditations, necessarily transformed into broodings, had worn him out, since what he was trying to think up was inconceivable and could not even be brought to mind. Those who are not satisfied that we exist in reality and *really* are, just because others say so and act like people who really believe that they live in a really believed world—those who take up this revolt are no longer able to adjust. They are ultimately compelled to become mockeries to themselves and to the world, since they still wish to think the unthinkable. They are in a bad way, and the only forms of relief remaining to them are those like A.'s late search for his lost time.

To be sure, this relief was only needed by those who actually came from the absurdity of existence in the passage of time to the edge of a madness that is perhaps the only answer to what is not only the most tormenting question of being that can present itself to us, but the most deceitful one. We rack our brains in a search that leads to deep brooding and from there to pondering nonsense. Not to do so is to live in time and reality like Everyman: one is lulled into a kind of equilibrium that cannot be destroyed by anything but usually reconstructs itself in a kind of spiritual cell-renewal. One hangs between death and madness in a balance in which a spatialized chronological time and lived time have approximately the same weight and where the brain's inertia acts as a form of self-protection. Perhaps one claims to have a "natural feeling for time," a guarantee of a healthy mind and the strength to endure.

With this feeling, are we simply withdrawing from the danger zone of mental work into the comfort of convention? When we're not eavesdropping on ourselves, we do indeed speak fluently of time as if we knew all about it: tomorrow we'll see each other at twelve; a year ago I visited the Loire castles; waiting at the dentist is boring and time-consuming. Existence within society forces us to own a watch, to write down appointments in a notebook, to reserve a place on the ferry for a trip on a particular day across the English Channel. In the peace that comes with freedom from thinking, we have a past, present, and future, as they are expected of us because we are meant to be functional. But in the end, what's not questionable to us, precisely that "natural feeling for time" that we boast about and in whose certainty we know ourselves to be superior to anyone pondering nonsense, may still be different from comfort and acquiescence to the law of the functional. It actually has much more to do with "nature," we could argue, and not only with the nature of physical and mathematical order, derived from the science of reality, but with *lived* nature, *nature vécue*, to vary a concept familiar to us.

Because we *live*, certainly. It can be assumed we have a wound. At first, it will not close; it oozes pus and causes us pain, so that we notice it first as an attack from space outside of us, on our body, which we only fully possess when we don't, i.e., when we're not aware of it. But then it gets better. The struggle with the infection is won by the organism, the wound closes—and now, all at once, it is time that wipes out the injury. With each day that passes, the wound, healing up with new tissue, becomes more and more a lived time and lived nature, up to the day of time's triumph, on which, thanks to that time—said to heal all wounds, something which on the contrary, it does not do at all—this wound in fact no longer exists. The wound has become a scab, taken care of by time, and is itself not time any more nor even a spatial exterior, but simply a part of the body, no longer noticing itself and belonging to the world.

So obviously there really is such a thing as a natural feeling for time, one that goes beyond conventions that are operationally necessary. *But to meditate about time is not natural and is not intended to be so.* It is the work of human beings who are horrified, who are no longer at peace with themselves because their disquiet does not leave them in peace and they would like to find themselves by abandoning themselves, find themselves in the time whose secret one day distresses them in their aging and stirs them *up.* Is it because they've recognized that the healing of every wound is deceptive, since beyond every convalescence there stands waiting for them and everyone else the ultimate disability, after which no tissue renews itself any more? Is it because they cannot come to terms with the fact that they are now present in space and time but, on a certain day getting nearer and nearer they will no longer be there? The human beings who give themselves up to this dismay, even during a short hour of meditation about the time already gathered up in them, have in any case already partly left the space in which they can remain a bit longer. While their time passes by in the twinkling of an eye, they are still only creatures of time. Each of them says "I" and means "my time." And more and more they are becoming strangers to the others—to those who simply let time tick away, and even to those sharp-headed others who impose upon time the order of their well-functioning minds.

For the past few weeks, A. has been noticing, when she stands in front of the mirror in the morning, that little yellow nodes of skin or excrescences can be seen on her eyelids. They cause no further discomfort, don't hurt when touched, and can clearly be judged harmless. They're not even particularly ugly, just disfiguring in a very limited degree, only noticeable by others if they are explicitly pointed out. But for A. they add to a kind of uneasiness that has turned up in recent years, a new kind, without panic, yet still tormenting in a delicately insidious way. She consulted her small popular handbook of medicine, with which she concerns herself, to her own chagrin, more and more often, and concluded that she was afflicted with xanthelasma, something caused by certain deposits, especially the otherwise hated substance cholesterol, which her organism is apparently producing in increasing quantity. Xanthelasma also engenders, for a moment, an association with Xanthippe, which intensified A.'s discomfort, even though it was known to her that the reputation of the quarrelsome temperament, clinging to the wife of Socrates, was unjustified.

Thus A., fifty years old, calling herself with unbecoming humor Xanthippe because of her yellow disfigurements, practices in front of her mirror a business of self-assessment and illumination of the dark state of affairs of both alienation from herself and self-enrichment, of an aversion, even a resistance, to the ego flecked with yellow and looking back at her from the mirror, as she sometimes pompously says of herself, with "ravished" eyes. Since she is untrained in the work of the mind and feels both reduced and excited by this new hostility, it is understandable that she at first looks for assistance. One can look at it from whatever angle one likes, it's still a question of the failure of the metabolism, hence a manifestation of old age, and she turns for advice to Simone de Beauvoir, a writer she considers a friend even though they have never met, who has written so thoroughly and beautifully about *la force des choses* (the force of circumstances), especially the *condition of aging*. "I often stop, flabbergasted, at the sight of this incredible thing that serves me as a face," her friend writes. "I loathe my appearance now: the eyebrows slipping down toward the bags underneath, the excessive fullness of the cheeks, and that air of sadness around the mouth that wrinkles always bring. . . . I see my face as it was, attacked by the pox of time for which there is no cure."[1] A. mumbles: poor Simone, you who suffer without being a Xanthippe like me. —But she is still not entirely satisfied with her friend, even if full of sympathy, because although the latter has certainly complained, just as A. has, she has not described what still happens beyond or beneath the justified occasion for the complaint: that's what matters to A.

What is the basis for the delicately sawing pain that had already overtaken A. every morning in front of the mirror long before the yellow flecks appeared on her eyelids? It may be that somewhere, stored deep within her, there is a horror that for the present can't cope with aging and the organism's deterioration it causes; a deep fear of her ego, which at the same time is a non-ego. A. can still observe it, not only in the mirror but also by touching it. Thus, the hand that feels itself becomes in an uncanny way a feeling hand as well, the non-ego, so that constantly, even in youth, the most primally familiar thing comes before us as something alien. This shudder, part of our basic human condition, is indeed disguised by everyday life—(how bright or dark the new lipstick is; isn't the fashionable hairdo a little too bouffant; isn't the necklace just a nuance too indiscreet?)—so that one can step away from the mirror, tolerably poised, and present oneself to the day. But the thin everyday layer is ruptured whenever the aging human creature, seeking after the traces of its aging, remains fixed in front of its mirror image: then we are suddenly confronted with the horror that we are both ego and non-ego and as this hybrid can call our customary ego into question.

Yet perhaps the strongest weapon should still be kept in reserve along with "horror" and "fright" and the dramatic bombast that is immediately superseded for the aging by a disinclination for another kind of drama, less metaphysical, as it were, but therefore no less distressing, and one in which the bombast is also dissolved. A.'s eye fixes on the yellow skin excrescences. She does not like herself anymore, perhaps tells herself like her friend that what now has to serve as her face has become a dreadful thing. —Self-hatred? That would be going too far. Self-hatred always has a *moral* quality that cannot possibly be extended to an aversion for withered skin, to the cells of the tissue that gradually lose their soluble substances so that eventually the almost insoluble fundamental substance prevails. Self-disgust? Not even that: for A. knows very well that the xanthelasma and the withering skin have always been considered disgusting and probably even remembers dimly the aversion she herself had felt earlier for the decrepitude of others. But that knowledge has come to her essentially from outside, from the world in which her yellow flecks are those of a stranger, while this stuff is for *her*, even if she considers having it removed by a surgeon (by the way, how much does such an operation cost? is a competent expert available?). The flecks are still *her* flecks, her own, intrinsically hers, against which disgust can no more revolt than it can against her own metabolic discharge. Shame? Maybe. Although it would naturally be conceivable for all women and men, young and old, to go through the world with dried-out skin and soft colored nodules on their eyelids. Something like that would no longer be ugly, since it would be impossible in such a case for everyone to detest everyone.

But being tired of oneself: as an expression, it is comparable to "tired of life," a phrase that never conveys total hatred of life and disgust with life, even if it now and then leads to suicide, but always conveys a desire for life or a desire for a specific form of life that life has denied us. Tired of oneself, that's it.

The more she repeats the morning mirror experiment, which has become a ritual, the more A. discovers a parallel between being tired of herself and having a kind of self-satisfaction that resists acknowledgment. Something appears in her that is like the pride of having already endured for a long time so that, deeply mired in her weariness, she wears her brittle skin like a brave warrior wears his scars. Aging people have a narcissistic relationship with their bodies, except that the infatuation with the mirror image is no longer unequivocal but is precisely a weary love in which the weariness loves itself and the love is deeply weary of it.

Like everyone in her situation, A. wishes to throw light on this dark state of affairs, and she is astonished by the *ambiguity* in which she is transfixed and which has no chance of ever being reconciled to anything unambiguous. For the ambiguity extends not only to the paradoxical way she is both weary and satisfied with herself in front of the mirror; even the dissonance caused by the combination of alienation from, and familiarity with, herself, having come to be the total harmony in her life, causes her trouble.

She has become a stranger to herself, for sure: what she witnesses in her morning ritual has nothing or only a little to do with the external self she drags along with her from her earlier and even later better days, for she still always likes to say of herself in a justifiably lofty level of consciousness that she "feels young." Her name, when she reads it on an envelope, brings to her the association of a not yet aging woman. She refers to her friend and finds herself again: "When I read in print 'Simone de Beauvoir,' it is a young woman they are telling me about, and who happens to be me. . . ." It is no different with A. Perhaps the strongest component of her weariness is just this alienation from herself, this discrepancy between the young self she has brought along with her through the years and the self of the aging woman in the mirror. But in the same breath and in the same tick of time it becomes obvious to her, if she just perseveres in front of the mirror and does not turn away from the glass, irritated as only a stranger can be, that she, along with all the yellow flecks and lackluster eyes, is *closer* to herself, with all her weariness and intimate familiarity, than ever before, and that in front of her mirror image, now a stranger to her, she is condemned to become more and more oppressively herself. —"I had the impression once," wrote her friend, "of caring very little what sort of figure I cut. In much the same way, people who enjoy good health and always have enough to eat never give their stomachs a thought. While I was able to look at my face without displeasure, I gave it no thought, it could look after itself. The wheel eventually stops, I loathe my appearance now." A., however, different from her friend or at least different from the way she described it, knows that she not *only* detests her face, that it is not *only* alienated from her. For once, when this countenance that one could not look at without pleasure was a matter of course, when one could "forget" it—did it exist for her at all? It had been a part of the world to which she belonged and which belonged to her, part of a self that, without contradiction and without ambiguity, was both self and world, one that did not doubt itself since it was not yet alienated from itself. Only now, in this transformation which, it seems to her, sometimes goes as far as being unrecognizable, only now is this strange visage, no longer focused on the world because it's been expelled from the world, completely hers: this discovery of the clasping together of alienation from oneself and an increased sense of self, whose extreme case may be a narcissistic melancholy, is the fundamental experience of all those aging persons who simply have the *patience* to persevere in front of the mirror, who can summon up the courage not to let themselves be chased away by yellow flecks and dehydration, who do not internalize the conventional judgment of others and submit to it. —A. will continue to carry out her ceremony before the mirror until the day in which she will either be removed from space or have become, instead of an aging woman, an old woman who no longer preserves any ego from her earlier life and who must look for her former appearance in her photo album.

It is the ambiguity of aging that A. is discovering and in which she is establishing herself, not just a matter of self-exploration in front of the mirror. The relationship of an aging human being, of a woman or a man, to his or her body is ambiguous in every situation of life. For aging is not a "normal condition" for the aging person: a norm is a matter of objective insight. That applies to aging just as much as to death, which for every other person is also just a fact and nothing else. A seventy-five-year-old lady whose body was still in good condition went to a specialist about the rheumatism that was tormenting her. Again and again, she explained in tones of angry indignation that she had never had the disease before and now the doctor should please charm it out of her body. The physician, who was in a joking mood, said, "Why, yes, gracious lady, and when did you actually want to have your rheumatism if not now?" The lady did not understand the joke at all: she did not want to have rheumatism, not at any stage of her life, just as she did not wish to get old and to die, age and death being events that affect others. We find it in good order if our neighbor ages and dies: ourselves we always remove from the course of life and death.

For all those who do not let themselves blend into a social consensus, who do not adapt a general opinion—which is really only an opinion about opinions—aging is no more of a normal process than rheumatism was for the old lady. Actually, it is quite definitely a sickness, indeed a form of suffering from which there is no hope of recovery. It is probably true that we also get sick as aging human beings and then, in the sense of medical science, become "healthy" again. Yet, as we age, we constantly find ourselves at a lower point of the organic spiral after we have recovered: we are never as healthy as we were before, no matter how gratifying the information of the doctor might sound. Today we are somewhat less healthy than we were yesterday and a measure more healthy than we will be tomorrow. Aging is an *incurable* sickness, and because it is a form of suffering it is subject to the same phenomenal laws as any other acute hardship that afflicts us at some particular stage of life. By incorporating familiarity with one's own body and estrangement from it, aging establishes the same relationship with our body that a specific indisposition has, bringing us illnesses in increasing number and of growing destructive power, while still, as a whole and even during phases of relative physical well-being, having the character of the hardship that characterizes every lighter and heavier sickness. In aging, which still allows us to be ready for revolt even while the age we've already attained is disparaged in resignation, we are conscious of our *condition*.

Indeed: it's a rather cheap truth to say that our condition generally gets noticed only when we are out of condition. Of course, anyone who needs to say, "I feel good," is not entirely comfortable with himself, just as the man who maintains that he feels young can never be a really young man. Whoever thinks about feeling good or bad cannot really be in very good shape, because as long as we are actually in full possession of our powers and continue to live in the certainty of a healthy bodily condition, we don't think about how we "feel." We are not with ourselves— but, as we can read in the writings of a great German physician and anthropologist,[2] we are "there," along with the things and happenings of the world; we are, to add to the physician's remarks, *outside of ourselves*, in space that is part of us and belongs to us, that is intimately and inseparably bound up with our egos.

The aging, however, come more and more to a worldless ego, partly becoming *time* through the past gathered up by memories of mind and body, and partly becoming more and more their own body. In that they fare just like our A. in front of the mirror—even when she avoids her mirror image like the many aging people who have accepted the value judgment that the wizening of age is ugly—: she perceives her body, which at this stage is present to her as her ego, as a shell, as something external and done to her, and at the same time as something that is actually hers, to which she is more and more reduced and to which she devotes increasing attention. We like to sidestep the mirror. But we cannot keep from seeing the hands on which our veins protrude, the stomach that is getting flabby and foldy, the feet whose toenails have become thick and cracked. We cannot run away from our body, even if blind; we cannot get out of our skin, no matter how much we would like to, whenever we touch this flaky, scaly skin. The body, which, as Sartre has said, was once *le négligé* and understood itself by *not* understanding—this body, which is no longer the mediator between the world and us, but cuts us off from world and space with its heavy breathing, painful legs, and the arthritically plagued articulation of our bones, is becoming our prison, but also our last shelter. It is becoming what remains, a shell—the phrase "mortal remains" probably suggests itself to every aging person who reflects upon what is happening to his or her body—but becoming in the same breath of thought the most extreme human authenticity, since in the end *it* is what is finally right.

Whatever was earlier world, as part and portion of our ego, shrinks with and through the withering body: it becomes the clear negation of us ourselves.

For a few years, A. has been disturbed by the cooling off of what he once called his feeling for landscape. Mountains, valleys, forests he once loved are now, to him, a club into which he has not been admitted. There's no doubt he has good enough reason to be skeptical about interpreting nature as an aesthetic landscape: at certain times very close to the present, forests, valleys, and mountains were the butt of bad poetry and even worse politics. Those who once called themselves "tied to nature" and sang of the landscape with rather rasping voices were the enemies of the human. A. would have a reason to stick with Signor Settembrini when he explained to life's young problem child[3] in his graphic words how nature in its relationship with the mind is the evil principle and belongs to the devil. Yet for A., the Italian friend of the intelligent word is a pleasant literary memory, but no authority, and he knows very well how senseless it would be to deny himself the pleasures of the contour of a mountain or the undulations of a forest slope just because a short but still historically very distant time ago, a most suspicious kind of aesthetics of the landscape and mystification of nature had existed.

It lasted a good while before he got to the bottom of his loss of a feeling for landscape, a loss that was about to coalesce negatively in a pronounced displeasure in landscape. Specifically, he became conscious in nature more than in the city of how the world, which he still had possessed as a part of his person, had become the denial of this person.

The mountain, laborious to climb, even if it was to be climbed at all, was by this time his anti-ego. The water in which he wanted to swim, but which he only endured when it had a quite specific temperature that it certainly would not have, said no to him. The valley, charming but full of flies that had never bothered him at all in his youth but now irritated him with rage, became the negation of his expansive desires. The others climbed the mountain, swam in the lakes, strolled about in the valleys: he was expelled and thrown back on himself. The hostility of the landscape, which we present here only metaphorically, but which at the same time is a reality and an immediately given fact of consciousness in the *monde vécu*—it was only conscious to A.

now as the contradiction of his person. He began to avoid nature. Now he has become thoroughly alienated from it and withdraws to where the challenge of a world that has come to be his denial no longer humiliates him every hour: to his room. When friends invite him to Sunday excursions or sojourns in the country, he declines, thanking them indifferently. It doesn't make sense to match yourself against an opponent that incessantly increases in strength and superiority while you steadily decrease.

Reasonable scientific method or even just plain everyday observation will teach us that A.'s case is an individual one and, to speak in medical categories, the result of a deficient state of his health that does not allow him to pursue athletic or partly athletic activities, while everything else we are saying is overrefined drivel. —And isn't there also the example of the married couple, already deeply descended into age, still taking walks for substantial distances and feeling "good" and "young"? Certainly: the robust old ladies and gentlemen are still around, bestirring themselves for a little world and space. The one is a little sicker than the other; another is already aging noticeably at forty-five so that his erstwhile student colleagues hardly recognize him; still another remains so dauntless on her sixtieth birthday that her acquaintances find she hasn't changed at all and toast the sixty-year-old young lady. Beyond such self-evident truisms, however, what we were saying in trying to describe the essence of aging without going into either the sturdy nature of common sense or the objectivity of medical terminology is still *true*: that specifically the world does not only withdraw itself from those who are aging, but it becomes their adversary, and that everyone, sooner or later, afflicted with more or less deep bodily travail, gives up the unequal struggle and becomes disengaged. The day of the retreat with flags flying, of the total defeat by a world that's become hostile, comes for everyone—as certain as the death it heralds.

If there is something like a basic condition of aging, it can be approximately concentrated in words like "toil" and "trouble." Toilsome is the torpid half consciousness of the incurability of a malady; and troubling the certainty, not entirely acknowledged in most cases but always filling our existential space, that after each acute illness, while we may indeed perhaps regain our health in the medical sense, we still get up from the bed in terms of living our lives sicker than we were before. Here as well we are constantly in the clutches of the ambiguity of alienation from, and familiarity with, ourselves, of self-weariness and self-seeking. The former always drowns out the latter initially at the point where thought turns into speech: That's supposed to be who I am? they ask, those sick with aging and sick of it as well, whenever they look into the mirror or realize again and again while walking, running, or climbing that the world is becoming their adversary, that their body, which has carried them and their selves, is becoming a corpus that weighs upon them within and is itself a weight outside. In a deeper layer of what has been lived, however, prior to speech, the search for the ego and the addiction to it is preeminent. A peculiar course of events consummates itself there. The aging, whose physiques have forbidden them the world and maliciously compelled them to deal with this body itself, even ultimately to become body and nothing else, must inevitably experience the husk that will become their "mortal remains," both clothing them and disrobing them from within, as an externality— and the death threatening them as a murder.

The first stage of the dissociation of the ego in the aging process concerns the mental ego. In using that expression, we do not mean to speak of a transcendental ego but, on the contrary, are referring to one that consists of collected time, preserving its identity through memory—this ego of our consciousness would like to shed its husk in order to become itself again, i.e., that which it has constituted itself to be through memory. According to its feelings, it rebels against a false ego, into which our husk is trying to make us, this husk that consists naturally not only of an external husk but of inner elements as well, such as, for example, an aching stomach or a disturbed heartbeat. Perhaps A. says at that time, If only the damned cadaver would leave one in peace!—by which he thinks he can disengage himself from what is weighing upon him within and from what, visible for everyone to see, is wasting him away outside. And in fact the aging process is just such a materialization and substantiation. The metabolism, functioning more and more poorly, causes the entire organism to turn to dross in a process that is all-encompassing, externally recognizable, and subjectively noticeable. After a respectful distancing from the world of physical concepts, one might perhaps say that in aging the body becomes more and more *mass* and less and less *energy*. This mass, thoroughly perceived within them as such by those diseased with aging, stands in resistance to the old self, which has been preserved by time and has been constituting itself in time, as the hostile *new ego*, foreign and, in the exact meaning of the word, odious.

Still, the odious being engulfing us from within cannot always remain what it was. The old ego, if it continues to exist as accumulation of time, constantly becomes more and more absorbed in time (since world and space do withdraw) and enters into a kind of suspicious "gentlemen's agreement" with the new ego materializing in the burdensome body. Finally, a deeply suspicious symbiosis of memory linked to time's ego and the present of the body's ego emerges. An uncanny tenderness of the aging for their new ego turns up, a tenderness that in no way excludes their being tired of themselves but even accentuates it: A. touches a sore spot or looks hard and pensively at the way the skin on his leg is getting rough. What he indistinctly notices in deep ambiguity and contradiction and is scarcely able to advance to thoughts in words is something like this: You poor stomach that served me faithfully and digested what I took in so that I did not notice or even possess you, you who were concerned that the stream of humors in my body not run dry! You poor leg, you've been carrying me through a world of streets, mountains, cobblestones, and gas pedals! Now you've been taken from time and work and can't do any more; you're both tired, just like my heart that won't allow me anymore to go upstairs two steps at a time.

Miserable leg, wayward heart, rebellious stomach: you hurt *me*, you're my adversaries. I would like to touch you and look after you and commiserate with you and also to tear you out of my body and replace you. My head swims with the thought that I am my leg, my heart, my stomach, that I am all my living cells as well as those only sluggishly renewing themselves—and at the same time I am still *not* those cells. I am becoming a stranger to myself the more I approach them and, while doing so, becoming nonetheless myself.

In the vague metaphorical language we have chosen, for better or for worse, for our considerations, a language incapable of holding its own against scientific investigation, one can say: in aging, I am myself *through* my body and *against* it. I was myself when I was young *without* my body and *with* it. I will be, once I have passed over the stage of aging and enlisted in the army of the old, still only body and nothing else, body as progressive decrease in energy and increase in substance, until I become eventually no longer myself or anything else, as soon as my substance is ready to fall apart into its elements. Aging is—now let us overlook for once the fashionable word—the moment of the dialectical turn: the quantity of my body as it moves toward annihilation becomes the new quality of a transformed ego.

But what are we human beings? A dwelling place of excruciating pain, thinks A., as he wakes up one night with a toothache. Apparently a periostitis, brought forth by the flattening of the gum pockets, following which bacteria penetrate the jawbone. An excruciating pain attacks me so that the tooth supporting my bridge will probably be extracted. And then a skillful dental construction will collapse. After that, if I don't want to mumble my way through the world, prematurely senile, with a caved-in mouth, something that is unfortunately professionally impossible even though it would probably be the most comfortable solution, I'll have to have a dental prosthesis: extreme materialization of my already strongly materialized body. As I know from countless more or less witty jokes, the denture is not tragic, just comic. "In our youth you liked to bite me," the lecherous wife says to her husband, who murmurs something about his hard day at the office and is not disposed to the calamity of conjugal pleasure; but when she continues to seduce and demand that he once again become her seducer, he gives in, resigned, and says, "All right, all right, give me my teeth." —So much for the witty joke. A. is not in agreement with the person telling the joke. He finds that a denture is tragic like Lear on the heath and that anyone who cannot bite into meat anymore is sinking into a filthy misery. So life is obviously not only a dwelling place of the excruciating pain A. himself now feels in his jaw (so that he scarcely still knows where the drill has actually been applied, while something compels him urgently to want it somewhere else, perhaps next to the toothache), but also a grim place of mockery. Just as poverty is a disgrace and the majority of tourists find the sight of tattered fellahin unpleasant, so A.'s decay is obviously disgraceful: the world, meant here as a social complex, does not forgive us that the process of materialization is consummated in us right before its eyes; it is only interested in giving us good medical service and a cruel joke, both having come into being in society's wish to keep us off its back. While getting out of bed to get a glass of water and an analgesic, A. is thinking, I can try to do without world, mountain, valley, and street, neighbor, and joke-telling and commit myself more deeply to the pain that the deterioration of my body heaps upon me. To act as if it were nothing to wake up at night with a penetrating toothache and worry about having a denture does not work. Those who are brave, who don't want to know anything of their pain and want to dismiss it with a manly firm or a womanly enduring wave of the hand—not so bad, not so important!—they are assured of the respect owed to them by a society that does not want to be bothered by the spectacle of their demise. But nevertheless, in denying their pain and failing to recognize something that is their own, they never succeed in discovering themselves.

We only discover our body in pain and aging. Especially aging, in the way it heaps its burdens upon us more frequently every day. Since in its suffering it no longer transcends itself to dissolve in world and space, this body is just as much a true ego as the stratified time the aging have built up inside themselves.

Consequently, when A. now swallows the pain-soothing remedy and finds himself suspended between torment and hope for relief, making his confidence in being free from pain the only thing at all that opens up to him the possibility of reflective thought, he is determined to make use of the minutes of suspension and *enter into a relationship with* his toothache. It is, as he tells himself, *my* toothache: the desire to be rid of it, or to be next to it or to shove it on to his healthy neighbor through the crack in the door of the apartment, exists; still, the pain is in my jaw, the pain that tomorrow, like everyone else, I will probably entrust to the dentist, who can possibly save me by tearing something away from my ego with his hand armed with forceps and fit me out as a replacement with a *res extensa* of alien material, an increased feeling of my own self, a realization of my flesh in the self-denial of my flesh: it is both an addition to my ego and a loss of ego, specifically the forced sacrifice of a conventional, rather abstract ego that painlessly falls asleep and tomorrow will belong to the world, will be world.

Pain and sickness are the festivals of decay the body organizes for itself and for me. Their purpose is to ensure that I am absorbed in the body and consequently, through the inflammatory process, though certainly reduced in my ability to function, I am increased in what immediately belongs to me; I gain in ego.

The analgesic has its effect; relief sets in. A. breathes in deeply and escapes the problematic euphoria of pain which, besides, only took possession of him at the moment when he had already washed the remedy down and, along with it, had drunk the hope for freedom from pain. He falls back into the reactive realm of normality. He has been saved, like everyone who has been liberated from torment. It is bad to have bodily pain; it is good to be free of it. A. does not mourn after the gain in ego passed on to him by the toothache. What now sets in, in the moment of relief, is once again the feeling of alienation from his own self through physical deterioration, the signal of which was the pain in his tooth. What has become of me, he thinks, since his closed eyelids are already becoming heavy for him and he senses the approach of sleep. A person with defective teeth, an organism unable to put up any resistance to the penetration of microbes and their spread throughout his system. An aging person. Tomorrow the dentist, the forceps, the extreme materialization of my body in the form of a dentist for whom I will have to lay out a lot of money. Am I still that person who falls asleep here, saved from aches and pains but given over to other, more evil ones that will certainly still afflict me? Am I still that one? "Give me my teeth": that's how it will end before it ends. What an awful debacle. Sleep is good; to say "death is better" is senseless; the best would have been never to have been born: that is an empty formula that logic can easily dispose of.

Let's let this tooth-plagued person fall asleep; his thinking, becoming uncertain and giving itself up on the threshold of sleep, cannot help us further. In any case, what can be noted, beyond the nocturnal experience of our imagined person, is this: in the silent dialogue between self-gain and alienation from oneself, both of which the aging person experiences in toil and trouble, alienation is in the foreground, because the increase in ego effected by a painful substantiation of the body is experienced as such only at rare times, even if it can forever and ever be interpreted from specific symptoms, whether a particular person called A. apprehensively feels his aching limbs, whether he assumes the unpleasant custom of thoroughly telling others at length about his sufferings, or whether he quietly gives himself over to his aversion and becomes it. With respect to the new ego that has just come into being, only the feeling of being alienated can, for the most part, be intellectually realized.

Then, in the search for words to constitute the feeling of alienation, the aging may well think that the *res extensa* is gaining power over them and may side with the *res cogitans* rebelling against it. In other words, they think perhaps that the "mental ego," as their true ego, resists the assumption of power by the *physis* and is supposed to resist it. One of them, for example, takes a provocative stance and proclaims in high spirits, "I still will not let my asthma forbid me life." Then he stands—but who is this "he" anyway?—against this asthma, repudiates the *res extensa*, and does not accept his body. At this point, I confess that I am moving forward in these considerations only with great uncertainty, doubting my ability to make a thorough investigation. In fact, the only thing to investigate would be whether the Cartesian distinction between *res extensa* and *res cogitans* corresponds to a reality lived at the deepest level or whether it is not instead the case that they are both inseparably one and the same and precisely in their *souffrance vécue* victoriously resist every attempt at dissociating them. One would need to inquire whether the ego arrogantly rebelling against a non-ego, the "true" one, placed between quotation marks, the ego of the *res cogitans*, which also considers the decaying body as a non-ego and therefore loves to speak of the "damned stomach" and the miserably painful leg, really is *more* than just this stomach and just this leg. One would have to shed light on the tormenting and festive minute in which A. gave himself over entirely to his toothache as *his*, eventually becoming totally engrossed in its inflammation, and determine whether this was the authentic moment of truth.

These assertions clearly contradict everyday experience as well as the entire emotional infrastructure of the concepts of sickness and health. Otherwise, such considerations would have to result in human beings aspiring to the condition of sickness. But it is only a self-evident truth that this is not the case. We want to be healthy, not sick, we want to know we are young, not old, and normally we don't care in the least for the chance of gaining a greater sense of our ego through pain. But the reliance on a normality of thinking and feeling obvious to everyday experience can be of little use to us here. Normality is after all a socially operational concept, while we are actually making a possibly morbid attempt, still indispensable to our argument, to approach a lived subjective reality. We know that A., waking up at night with a toothache, threatened by forceps, extraction, and a thoroughly material false tooth, wanted to get rid of his piercing discomfort (otherwise he certainly would not have taken the soothing medication); we know that he was afraid of the dentist's intervention, still more so of the denture itself, looking as it did like a surrealistic sculpture. We know that A. became alienated from himself at this hour. We can also be just as sure that with his toothache he became himself in a new way. The small and harmless torture that stands here as an example of the burdens inflicted upon us by aging, even though every young person can obviously be afflicted with a toothache, has helped him to his, or at least a new, ego. The pain has made his own body, which is supposed to belong to the world, at least according to society and everyone's demand for social self-preservation, a possession that from now on is no longer to be shared with others. It has taken away from him one more piece of the world. Put differently, it has given him to understand in a crescendo that the world is his negation. In this case, it is society that is left in the lurch, not knowing where to start with a fellow who, regardless of loss of world and gain of ego, is not capable of filling out his income tax declaration because of his toothache.

Who has the last word? The body that brings to the aging a new familiarity with themselves? Or the society that imposes on every human being an ego that has to stay healthy, i.e., operational, and that as *res cogitans* opposes the bodily ego absorbed in the *res extensa*? The question is hardly answerable. In any case, we have to limit energetically what we have said about the moment of truth in which the bodily ego is unveiled to us by pain as the true one. That's because the mental ego, which the aging carry within them and which in memory is lived time, has in fact constituted itself through the reaction of fellow human beings to our existence. But in the end, that mental ego always turns out to be the stronger, and we eventually come back by detour to the results of superficial everyday experience and to the concept of normality, referred to above in its limitations.

For we do not escape the look and the judgment of the others. As a young woman, A. once began a letter with *"mon chéri."* Since, however, the loved one was at that moment no longer the man who loved her, the *"mon chéri,"* placed in the world without any social, fellow-human, or communicative legitimacy, grew pale and expired. A. was essentially an abandoned woman, regardless of how it might have been with her body and her mind, and this bit of abandonment was a part of the ego she later recalled in memory along with her earlier days of triumph when the *mon-chéri* letters she wrote were justified and were granted their rights by the *ma-chérie* letters from her friend. Since there is no choice now but to accept the ego as a social coordinate, the alienation from oneself felt by the person sick with age is ultimately not only more persistent than the gain in ego achieved through the pain and materialization of the body, but also more determining, more real, if that's the way it is, since it is the real that has had, and has, an effect.

It had an effect thanks more to the others than to the body, for even the body of suffering, especially, is entrusted to them. Furthermore, the effect one has clutches after the others, since it can't happen without them. What we were saying is true—and let nothing be taken back from it—: that A.'s disgust with the yellow flecks is imposed upon her from outside, from learning specifically that such disfigurements appear disgusting to those who are not disfigured, even while the deformity is still *her* possession, A.'s, which to her cannot be primarily abhorrent. But world and life would add that it is not a question of primacy. The social ego, even if imposed upon us by society, is just as much something of our own as anything that immediately and physically experiences itself.

Society does not know what to do with a person like A., plagued by a toothache till his thoughts are confused. Little avails him when, suspended between torment and the hope for relief, he euphorically experiences his ego's moment of truth. He must comply. What we call reality is a force field of social tensions, actions, and reactions. Its ego-building force does not release us as long as we exist. The imposed ego is in the end simply the ego pure and simple, and it takes an ego dissociation of an unusual kind to discover beyond our socially defined ego the one given by the body and only by the body. The ambiguity of alienation from oneself and familiarity with oneself in aging—by which we must not forget for one minute that aging is a form of suffering and that we experience it as such—this ambiguity therefore consists not only in the fact that we feel our body as a mortal shell while at the same time this shell is taking new root in us more and more; it also becomes manifest in our social ego's contradiction of everything else that is formed from our suffering body, of the body-ego that is both our clothing and what we clothe. A. does not know where to go with the decrepit body that causes him toothache and from which eventually his tooth will fall out. To be sure, he can start a relationship with his pain and acquire something he could perhaps call his "knowledge." But such is only possible during the night: not only because society demands that he fill out the income tax declaration free of pain and with a clear mind, but also because he cannot accept the ego of toothlessness, refused by the world and expelled from it, that threatens him. For he is "world" himself, he is society, and he sees himself with the latter's eyes. A. himself thinks he senses that society senses him: therefore, he wants to preserve the ego of fresh teeth he's dragged with him from his youth and at any price get rid of the other ego he called in the middle of the night his "authentic ego."

Which ego do we carry over out of the past into aging? We were sitting on the school bench at ten. We kissed at twenty. At thirty, we advanced, envied by our colleagues, into our profession, and as forty-year-olds, we discovered that the other sex still liked us. At each time we were an ego. To what kind of ego do we cling in aging, knowing or only imagining that only in this one we were more *ourselves* than in any other afterward or before? One person had rich wavy hair as a young man. Now, disheveled but proud, he wears the graying tufts remaining under his bald pate on the sides of his temples as a picturesque hair ornament. Another thinks she remembers that at thirty she was charming to the world of men because of her well-developed bust. Accordingly, she still prefers, at fifty-five, deep, low-necked *décolletages*, even though the skin at the top of her cleavage is already flaccid and brownish. In truth, the man with the disheveled tufts was not admired as a young man for his natural undulations, but for his witty conversation, and the *décolletée* lady once owed her successes not to her well-built breast but to her intelligent, lively eyes.

It is true that the ego we carry with us is a creation of society. Even here there is nothing to take back. Still, in the act of remembering, we have *remodeled and newly interpreted* our social ego. The ego that we set as our own against the deterioration of aging, this ego that we believe we have to look at and sense in relation to our new, yellow-flecked or dentally endangered, even foreign and offensive, ego has sometimes not existed in reality at all. The alien image of ourself is a vague statistical reality: five hundred others showed their antipathy toward us; only a minority of fifty were inclined to put up with us: therefore we were disliked only in a "reality" written in quotation marks. What's bad about all this is that we do not know the statistics. We don't know that our social ego was not only built up by the others but for the most part may have come into being through mere supposition. The reality of the social ego we experience as such every day and to which we submit is in the end just as questionable as A.'s nocturnal toothache ego. It may sometimes seem to agree approximately with statistics unknown to us, but there is no relying on that. In aging, we become alienated from ourselves, doubled and inscrutable, for when A. says, shaking her head in front of the mirror, "That's not me any more," the subject is as little known to her as the predicate.

The consequence of such considerations would be that an ego, since it is still multifariously dissociated in the suffering of aging— dissociated into the body I have, the "other" that painfully has *me*, into the *res cogitans* and the *res extensa* of my own self, into the ego, questionably deduced from the reactions of my fellow human beings, which we preserve as lived time, and into the daily changing ego of aging—the absurd consequence of trying to find out in this manner about our most inner conditions would be that a lived ego, a *true* identity, does not exist. One can set that aside as a bare and worthless mental game, for ego dissociation is in every moment counterbalanced by ego association. The question about the reality of the ego is a sham question—: just as Ernst Mach's proposition that the ego is a bundle of feelings was a sham proposition because the very act of bundling canceled the individual elements of the bundle as such. We refer to the ego when we say "I," and we say "I" with good reason and good sense even if we like to stand in front of the mirror shaking our heads and doubting ourselves, even if at night we like to entrust ego-building power only to pain, even if we recognize that the image of ourselves we've carried with us is imposed upon us by society without us ever knowing in this case whether this too is a hallucination of our speculation. Finally, it is still the case that our skin surface demarcates us: what transpires on this side of the boundary is what we are; what happens beyond it is other. A phenomenological way of perceiving, eschewing the opposition of inner and outer and adapting space to us and us to space so that I am myself as much as my world of space, strikes at the core of what has been lived and yet aims right on past it. It is true that at the level of what has been immediately lived we are both "we" and "world." It is just as true that at that same level we constantly make distinctions. In the *monde vécu* and in the attempt to reconstitute it mentally, the basic propositions of logic no longer hold, that's the *misère*. The ambiguity becomes an antinomy.

And yet: we have to take logical contradictoriness upon ourselves, have to take upon ourselves absurdity and the risk of every mental confusion when we meditate on our condition. *It is aging that exposes us to that kind of consciousness and makes us capable of it.* By this time, the world whose image is logic is already clearing out.

When we have crossed the top of a mountain and begin to go down the other side and it quickly becomes steeper and steeper, faster and faster, it is no longer our place to think in a way appropriate to the conquest of the world, feeling compelled to demonstrate for ourselves an image of the world in logic. The primal contradiction, death, awaits us and compels us to form logically unclean propositions such as, "When I no longer am." Death is already in us, making room for equivocation and contradiction. We become I and not-I. We possess an ego enclosed in our skin and may at the same time find out that the limits always were fluid and stayed that way. We become more alienated from ourselves and more familiar with ourselves. Nothing is self-evident anymore. The evidence is no longer believable. Alienation from oneself becomes alienation from being, no matter how faithfully we still attend to the day, fill out our tax declaration, go to the dentist. Were we saying that in aging the world becomes our denial? We could just as easily have said that we are already about to be the negation of our self. Day and night cancel each other out in twilight.

# The Look of Others

A novel to recommend to readers getting on in years: *La Quarantaine* by Jean-Louis Curtis. It is not a great book, but a reflectively beautiful one about the fate of two married couples at the peak of their lives. Ingeniously, its title plays with the double meaning of the word *quarantaine*, whereby on the one hand the decade of aging between forty and fifty is meant, on the other the hygienic isolation imposed upon human beings, no longer young: their quarantine.

The provincial notary André, a distinguished patrician from the Pyrenees, a man of means and some culture, finds himself after many years once again in Paris, but for the first time without family dependents. This man on the threshold of fifty puts up at the Ritz, a small, sentimental, and expensive homage to Marcel Proust. In the first evening, he tries the Lido on the Champs Elysées. The girls are attractive, the jazz is good; afterward he is alone in his hotel room and looks down at the Place Vendôme, which, since he had last seen Paris, has turned into an autodrome.

He intends to devote the evening hours of the next day to the theater where a critically acclaimed play of the Brecht school is running. In the midst of the performance, the boredom that was still amorphous yesterday and that he did not admit to himself becomes manifest. Vexed, he leaves the theater after the second act. The venture of a walk turns into a debacle. The offensive smell of exhaust fumes takes away his breath and makes the *flânerie* he had looked forward to for weeks impossible. He seeks refuge in a café, but even that proves to be hopeless; neither in the Flore nor in the Deux-Magots is a place to be found. A. could accept all that if he did not increasingly have the feeling that he is *invisible*. No one notices him. It seems, he thinks, that you don't exist in this city if you're older than twenty-five. The next morning he takes his departure in deep depression. A few weeks later, he suffers a heart attack.

It can be said that A.'s case is a very personal one, not valid for the immense majority of his comrades in aging: his feelings of invisibility or insignificance are to be explained from a totally individual and incidental morose mood, perhaps even from sensing in advance his physical condition. But as a rejoinder, one can raise the objection that his defeat at Paris has only a little to do with the contingency of his person, that instead it is inscribed in the social and economic structure of an era in which a person, both driven and lashed into mere matter by the demands for production and expansion, has recognized that only youth is fit for work and pleasure and that in general what is popularly known as idolatry of youth is the prevailing disposition. The argument has weight. The facts of society speak for it, those facts that can be read out of such simple publications as the job-offerings in the newspapers: those who are sought—the editors-in-chief, directors, chief engineers, and whatever the terminology of the second half of the twentieth century calls "managers"—are not supposed to be older than forty. But we're not concerned here, not yet at least, with the professional fate of the aging and old people who are becoming more and more numerous in a world in which every day less is known about what to do with them. We want to consider the problem of *social age* in general, meted out to us by the look of the others. Beyond that, we want to consider our destiny as individual human beings who can live neither without others nor with them or against them, and the absurd and contradictory basic constitution of human beings who, as individuals, would like to reign over their property—the world!—and at the same time know that world and property only exist where others dispute their right to place and possession. Even this contradiction, like most of those that mar our existence, only becomes fully conscious to the aging person.

What does "social age" mean? In the life of every human being there is a point in time or, to be more mathematically precise, the vicinity of a point where each discovers that one is only what one is. All at once we realize that the world no longer concedes us credit for our future, it no longer wants to entertain seeing us in terms of what we *could* be. Society no longer brings the possibilities into focus that we still think are vouchsafed to us in the picture that it makes of us. We find ourselves—not through our own judgment but as the mirror image of the look of the others that we immediately internalize—to be creatures without potential. No one asks us any longer, "What do you want to do?" All declare, dispassionately and unflinching, "*That* you've already done." The others, so we have to learn, have struck a balance and laid before us a bottom line that *we are*. One of us is an electrical engineer and will remain so. Another is a post office administrator who maybe can still become the director of his office with some effort and luck, but that is all. Another is a painter, unsuccessful or successful: if success has congealed in a sum of living and creative events, it will remain faithful to her even if there are deviations in the art market and the prices quoted for her pictures today are possibly not as high as yesterday; however, if success, that which follows from her efforts, the effect of her art, has not been forthcoming, then it is the lack of success, the negation of her artistic existence, that characterizes her. Whoever A. is, A. will not become a big game hunter if he or she has not done so already, nor a political leader, nor an actor, nor a professional criminal. That which we call our "life," the sum of what we have done and left undone, defines what we likewise still regarded as our life yesterday, that is, the years that are at best still left to us. Those we can already foresee as the homogeneous and monotonous repetition of our wasted time.

It is probably true that only death makes a clean break; only the end of a life gives the truth to its beginning and all its stages. The game—theoretically—is never played before it is played *out*. There may be break-ups, new beginnings, upheavals, and outbursts, so that in the end a stage lived in numbness and petrification can unveil itself as a mere transitional phase. Gauguin. A bank employee refuses the bottom-line ego that society presents to him: his death on La Dominica expresses the truth about the existence of the bank employee and makes it nothing. How many Gauguins can be brought forth as witnesses? In the future, in a world defining itself by social function through interaction and interdependence, there will be even fewer who can break out. The bottom-line egos, results of the balance struck by social fusion, will be accepted, internalized, and eventually required. Human beings are what they socially accomplish. The aging, whose accomplishments were already counted and weighed, have been condemned.

They have lost even if they've won, that is, even if their social existence, completely consisting of their consciousness and consuming it, is assessed at a high market value. Break-ups and upheavals no longer lie on their horizon; they will die as they lived, each a soldier and brave.[1]

One has to ask about what it is that inheres in the verdict of society and what chances offer themselves to dismiss it. The judgment passed during our active life by a consensus taking shape unnoticeably in our minds is never finally given. Our social existence, which is our existence plain and simple as soon as we have entered the phase of aging, is recorded in a dialogue. We speak, society answers. What we do and perform is the first act of a social reality. The second act, radiating back to the first and in that way giving its dimension, is a reply to, or action against, the first. We think we speak as poets—it can be assumed—and challenge society with our poetic word. Whether we were effective enough to be poets in reality will depend upon whether society accepts our challenge.

This game, in the many meanings of the word—a play in the theater of the world based on its ending, pure *ludus*, a game of chance with the highest stakes—is neither won nor lost as long as we are young. We beat on the doors today and no one responds, but tomorrow they will open up to us—so we hope and believe, since the belief and hope of society are part of us, and no fellow human beings would like to be deaf to the knocking on their door. Once we are aging and have already gathered in a large number of answers, once society has already applied an inventory of the rejoinders issued to us, only then does that same society feel certain of its newly imparted information and calculates it automatically according to the inventory sum. Those who do not open their doors then no longer risk the role of being deaf to others. At the same time, it is certain that they have heard in our knocking the voice of what has been. Now the dialogue has ossified into a uniform litany that will only end with our end. We ask the eternally same questions because we get the eternally same answers, and we preserve the latter because the former always stays the same.

It would be good to know whether it is not perhaps possible to escape the judgment of society (which, because of its opaque, quantitatively demonstrable massiveness is also a verdict), even to elude it in aging and in old age where it has thickened to become impenetrable. "Who are you?" the mental doctor is asking the patient. "Talleyrand." Talleyrand shakes in the prison clothes fluttering around his body like a fool's dress, shuffles in his slippers, spoons his soup out of his wooden bowl. He is still Talleyrand: the verdict of society does not concern him. Or the great painter A. in the Café du Dôme at Montparnasse. His name cannot be found in any reference work; he has not exhibited anything in ten years; art galleries do not like hanging his pictures even in their side rooms. "Who are you?" "I am a great artist, but you have to understand, the market place, industry, fashion, everything is against me." The verdict of society can be dismissed through the total eclipse of the whole scene, that is, through denying the same reality principle that Talleyrand rejects in the mental institution. One can even arrange one's refusal by obscuring a section of the stage as the painter A. does with the narrow world of his profession. But neither Talleyrand in the madhouse nor the painter A. has a social age. They beat on doors, indefatigably, and don't care in the least that no one opens to them. They talk into the void and give up all claim to a response. Society tells them, "If you were what you claim to be, great painter and Talleyrand, we would have to know it." They don't hear anything, the verdict does not reach them.

The number of lunatics is slight. Even those who are a half or a quarter crazy are not many. Most are "normal." In our case, that means that at a certain age they accept society's judgment. When they were young, they again and again tested themselves, more or less courageously (that is a matter of individual disposition), in going beyond a possible limit, possible precisely because society still recognized it as such. But in aging, their reality is their age, the social age that concerns them just as much as the age of layers of time stored up in their memory or that other age that is experienced by them as loss of the world through the toil and trouble of a deficient *physis*. Generally, this social age cannot ever be defined, it depends on the epochs, the social structures, the respective field of relationships to which a person is yoked.

When Kennedy became President of the United States at forty-three, he was young; a forty-three-year-old assistant professor is not young. Or the other way round: Senator Thomas Buddenbrook in Thomas Mann's novel *Buddenbrooks*, who gained his senatorial rank when he was around forty, was precisely by virtue of this dignity and its patriarchal aura a very mature man, almost aged. His dissolute brother Christian, with the indefinite pain in his leg and the propensity for champagne breakfasts, was, even on his deathbed, a boy who had become senile too early. Social age is defined by a network of causality, much too complicated to be disentangled here. Our very own social ambitions form one of its numerous skeins. A subordinate official, for example, is socially an old man at forty-five when, and only when, he has tried to attain a higher position. As long as he never tries to rise in the hierarchy, has never spoken of his hopes for advancement either with his family, with his friends, or with his superiors, his social age is not defined and not definable. In his subordinate position, there is no social relevance in being thirty or fifty. He lives on in his position without history, a man without biography—and only the weight of memory or his burdensome body lets him become aware one day that he is aged. In agreement with his own modest ambition society had already passed judgment on him when he was still very young in years. To be socially ageless or even old from early on, that doesn't matter now; right up to his end he takes things as they come.

If there are criteria in our time for social age that go beyond all structural, national, and individual differences, if we can delimit the vicinity of the point at which our social judgment receives its full validity and the world no longer allows us to go beyond what we have judged to be possible, we find our orientation in the realm of *possession*, to which the market value we may represent also belongs. For our homeland is not a world of being but one of having; more exactly, a world of being that is only given through having. What one is, what one stands for, is defined by what one has. Human beings are required to have, according to common and accepted principles of order—a computable possession or a possession representing and guaranteeing market value—and they enter into the phase of social aging as soon as they *do have*. If they don't have anything, they've perhaps been spared social aging. Still they have to learn that neither social essence nor humane existence has been conceded to them. Born dumb, nothing more learned; born poor, nothing more earned. They then have neither social standing nor permanence; they're an imaginary Talleyrand or garret genius. The society of having neutralizes autonomous individuals who, under pressure of the requirement of having, can no longer hold up against the look of the others the prospect of a personality wanting to be itself.

One may take one's orientation from the signs and markings along the path of having possessions—and then have a hard time locating the points of reference for aging. For the fact of having possessions or the requirement for them affects us at quite different phases of our life. For one person, the fate of having possessions begins very early, in the cradle, if he's born as an heir and the paternal factory or legal chancellery awaits him, presses upon him, long before he is yet conscious of himself. For another, the process begins in the higher levels of school where a gift for mathematics urges her into the career of a physicist or an engineer, certain of her market value. For a third one, it happens at the university or in the first years of professional practice. In any case, however, having dictates an existence that structures one's consciousness and is in two ways a destiny: on the one hand it robs us of our own disposability, of the possibility of beginning anew any moment at point zero and designing our lives with our own will without society or even against it. On the other hand, by withdrawing or gathering itself together as the possession of economic resources or as a definite ability, a "know-how," required by society and honored through its market value, it condemns us to remain an empty place in society, a hollow form without even the ability to plan for our zero point, society already having disposed of that ability.

With every day, the world of having admits fewer and fewer outsiders who can plan for themselves.

The integrating power of having is very great. The possessions or the market value of a single individual makes that person all the more flexible, since those things are chains worn as agreeably as jewelry is worn.

A. is a forty-year-old journalist who composes articles on consignment. His skill, his alert pen, as his customers call it with approval, has assured his written product a definite commercial value. He is living. Not exactly in luxury or in security, but also not

in need and not in anxiety about abject misery. He writes and sells
what he's written, has a fairly decent house, drives a car, takes vacation trips. Sometimes, before falling asleep, he is plagued with
memories: he was sitting in a garret, a zero. He did not think anything he wrote would ever find a buyer, and therefore he noted
down whatever he wanted and how he wanted it. What kept him
alive was the wide horizon: since he was nothing, he was everything. His potentiality was the whole world and all of space. In the
realm of the potential, he was world revolutionary and *clochard*,
pimp and philosopher. He was young. He was young in his years
and in his body, and if he had space before him, then it was because not very much time had been gathered up in him yet. But
he was also young in his social existence, younger than the M.D.
of the same age who was just treating his first patients to death or
the actor who was pasting his first critical reviews in a scrapbook.
Now he is not that anymore. Now he *is* because he *has*, no matter
how little it might be. Society has allocated his social age to him
after it first let him know that it only tolerates an eternal youth in
the madhouse. He has his social age, and sometimes he feels with
deep horror his agreement with it. To be a taxpayer and a citizen
whose greeting the neighbors return on the stairs of his apartment
building! The sum of a number of humiliating capitulations fills
him for the moment with a silly pride. He is ashamed that he has
come to this point and that his existence without having, the existence of permanent becoming, has been stolen from him by an
existence prescribed by having. Then he asks himself whether it is
possible to think of a social order in which his ridiculous victory
(which is a sad defeat) could have spared him. It would be a
system in which existence is not having something, not even
having knowledge (perhaps because having knowledge would not
be translatable into a category of possession), but would remain an

existence of becoming: to be and to become with the others whose look would not overpower him, but instead would help him again and again to be zero and to constitute himself anew starting from the zero point. A. asks himself about this and finds no answer and knows that it is very likely that his not finding an answer was already determined in the successive acts of his capitulations and in what he has had all around him. He has already become engrossed in these things, no matter how slight they may be, and because he has them he can no longer not want to have them. Like countless others with the same fate, he has chains to lose that can be worn as easily and agreeably as the adornment of a destroyed existence that ruins itself humanly even as it builds itself up socially. He has aged. Society bears the blame. He bears the blame himself to the same extent that he accommodates himself to what society has set instead of becoming a fool or bleeding to death like Che Guevara.

Guevara, Gauguin, the megalomaniac in the madhouse and his distant relative in the Café du Dôme, they are not affected by the look of the others, the look that represents the world of having possessions. Nor, for that matter, are the nabobs whose property is so great that it does not mean anything to them anymore and does not determine who they are. Ali Khan drove to his death young, and the Duke of Windsor will die like Christian Buddenbrook, boyish and senile. The others reach a social age, sooner or later, most of them at a point in time at which they present themselves to society as producer-consumers worthy of investment. At some time, they have something they own to defend, acquired knowledge to offer, a marriage partner to care for as well as children. Defined by what they have and wanting to increase or preserve it, both exhausting the whole person, they stick it out and become one day aware of turning a corner beyond which their existence based on having cannot be called back: then they are aging persons. The doors will not be opened any more. Whoever directs a question to society gets an answer: keep on with what you were doing yesterday and the day before, do whatever your past compels you to do—or do nothing. Wanted: experienced banker to take over our branch office, maximum age: 40; business person well versed in textiles with knowledge of English capable of reorganizing our business, no older than 45; young, dynamic, forward-moving and energetic individual, likes to work, good personality, traveling agent, laboratory manager, engineer, editor, publicity agent. The heads of personnel have the look of the other, requiring not only a social age that corresponds to the logic of investment, but, it is clear, experience in a particular profession. They won't employ a beginner at the age of forty. Their contemporary X., who from twenty-three to forty has computed foreign exchange rates, calculated working hours for piecework, drafted advertising posters, or written articles on consignment will do the same for two to two and a half decades more. He asks himself sometimes when he looks up from his work, Is this to go on forever? and feels his anxiety. It will go on like this, not exactly forever, but still for an eternity of his existence; as long as his forgetful brain, his heavy limbs, and the valid legal regulations permit it.

After that comes what society calls one's well-deserved retirement and what for one person means an ample administrator's retirement income, for another a miserable pension; but for both it means banishment from a reality being formed historically and confronting the very uncanny question: When have I actually lived? When did I stop leading my life as a process of constant renewal and permanent contradiction? Fortunately, such moments of questioning are rare.

These contemporaries, whether already pensioned or excitedly gesticulating individuals "in the midst of life," increasing what they have or maintaining it, accept the judgment passed on them by society, their social age. They are content with an ego that no longer tries to go beyond itself but that is not yet resting in satisfaction with itself, because the existential death contained in social resignation is just as unacceptable as physical death. It is still day, they say as they talk to themselves and want to be active like men and women. But the night has already set in, even before its actual entrance, and now they are only able to have an effect as society requires, allows, or forbids.

Something needs to be added here, especially about the metaphor of the night breaking in: it is a maudlin cliché, worse, it doesn't apply at all. Is it not so that the leaders and pillars of society are venerable persons, even all too venerable, and that the *ruling* generation is that of the fifty-five-to seventy-year-olds? Presidents and cabinet ministers, influential university professors, heads of boards of directors, members of learned societies, they are all getting on in years. On the other hand, whatever may concern all the other tiny nameless existences, society is already making its places ready for them. This is just a question of social engineering. A "meaningful life" and an old age worth living will be guaranteed in the future or at least made possible, in accord with the increase in life expectancy.

One shouldn't wax heroic about metaphors of twilight and the drama of aging. The days do get longer and longer for those who give orders, but also for the others who run alongside as fellow travelers. In our father's house there are many apartments and some of them look like well-furnished homes for the aged.

But a young physicist says, "The older men and women in our field enjoy official honors and the glorious dignity they've earned, but we, people between twenty-five and thirty-five, *we* make the discoveries." Behind the silver-haired captains of industry with their inexhaustible capacity for work—which the good old press tells us about—stand their prompters, the brilliant young men upon whom it all depends and before whose sharper intelligence the old bow in more or less good composure. More than ordinary people, the apparently powerful are subject to the verdict of society and are condemned by it to remain what they were. The titular chief executive officer of an industrial firm who has long since handed over his practical control to a group of young coworkers, the famous professor who has already been overtaken intellectually by a thirty-year-old assistant and now collects only distinctions and honorary doctorates, they play their prescribed roles just as precisely as any old man of magnificence speaking about great national questions in words of power previously heard and therefore easily manipulated: the latter and the former are prisoners of their past. Those in one group are no longer effective at all; the hackneyed night has in fact broken over them already; only their secretaries still fawn over them. Those in the other group may sulk like a bunch of Gorm Grymmes and flash like Jupiter; their speech and deeds are tied to the political roles through which they have acted previously. It was already night above the heads they carried high, too, even if brightened by the stars as well.

But what do the anonymous still hope for when their social age, their having-aged, is draped over them by society? The letter carrier remains a letter carrier just as de Gaulle remains *l'homme historique,* except that it is easier and better to portray one's own monument than one's own nothingness. But as soon as one is no longer even a letter carrier and has lost the ability to regard the delivery of a registered letter as an act of importance to the state, then nothing is left except waiting to see how to deal with the years of puttering around in a little garden. A "meaningful existence." Sure. Society may care for the aging with welfare or even by providing part-time work that doesn't really need to be done. They are not so stupid that they wouldn't know exactly that others are only letting them do as they like, that they are burdens and useless eaters. Perhaps they'll be cared for; that is of course better than leaving them to themselves and their meager pensions. If it did not sound so presumptuous, if it did not smack so pervasively of reactionary insolence, it could be added that their misery and their social isolation are still *their own* wrongs, constituting for them an ego—of grievance and accusation—while caring for them and providing for them make them into an other, even in their own eyes. This misery and isolation make them into creatures of total social determination, people who are no longer able to give even a bad conscience to those who are with them and those against them.

No one may doubt that social aging is essentially determined by the world of having. But it would be quite inadmissible to reduce the phenomenon of aging and being old, as it is determined by the look of others, to a few fundamental problems of social structure and of market and profit economics. Again and again we meet the fact of the body—the frail body in this case—which not only gives a specific color to the subjective quality of aging, but which first of all immediately releases the effects in society as well. You don't get prettier when you get older, said Erich Kästner once in a harmless poem. This trivial observation, which can neither be surpassed nor further reduced, is valid in all cases. One does not get more attractive, more agile, not even more clever, and the world—understood here as a statistically recordable sum of individual opinions, feelings, reactions—knows it and makes sure that it's well understood by the aging and the old, who today are not valued as rarities and therefore cannot be considered venerable images of divinity. Aging people get ugly: in German, ugly (*häßlich*) is that which one hates (*haßt*). They get weak, which in colloquial speech is the same as a value qualification, even an invalidation: one speaks of a weak play or a weak exchange rate and bestows ultimately on the weak human being just as little sincere sympathy as on a failed drama or a slump in securities. Numerous adjectives, all beginning with the syllable "un," are attributed to aging and old human beings: they are unable to perform much physical work, uncoordinated, unfit for this and that, unteachable, unfruitful, unwelcome, unhealthy, un-young. The negative prefix, as an expression of a negation welling up from deep emotional foundations, can be taken, if one likes, as the *negation* consummated by society, the an-nihilation of the aging human being. But the only thing that is an-nihilated here is what already bears the sign of nothingness on its brow, a nothingness whose graphic harbinger is physical decline. The undeniable aversion, converted into respect, of young people toward the old turns the respect for these elders into a mere convention. It is quite possibly a fear of nothingness, resistance to a way of not being that has already insinuated itself into existence.

The "world" an-nihilates aging human beings and makes them invisible on the streets, as is the case with the provincial notary A., who would like to stroll through Paris but cannot bring himself to do it anymore because he is rejected by the crowd that ignores him. The look of the others, which goes right through him as if he were a transparent substance, shatters him. He leaves the capital city and returns home to his small town in the Pyrenees, because in the long run his inconspicuousness becomes insufferable. It is the nature of human beings to aspire to exist for others. —That is all his literary creator, the novelist Jean-Louis Curtis, intended to say about his failed travel adventure. The book, *La Quarantaine*, says nothing about the disconcerting spectacle that the "world," while condemning A. to invisibility, still does not consist only of young people—there are also quite enough aging people crossing the boulevards on which the notary is annihilated by empty stares. It is good for the aging to realize that society, regardless of how it arranges the demographics of its age pyramid, accepts the annihilating judgment of the young and the most recent. Even the honors rendered to the aging, both private and official honors, change nothing about that. An aging person is old not only to youth but also to those of his or her own age who look at the young, too, even when they arouse no look in return. They deny solidarity to their comrades in destiny, try to maintain their distance from the signs of the negation of existence they read in their features. That is not to say that they love the young, only that they cling to them in an absurd longing and with an envy they cannot admit to themselves. Against the judgment, passed over the aging by young and old, but always according to the law of youth and its dread of decay, there is no appeal. Honors that serve as abundant testimonies to aging and old human beings are feeble and prove nothing.

Nothing, even when the veneration of the great old man is full of pomp and ceremony and even when the long applause of young hands clapping accompanies this curiosity of aging upon its entrance.

A. visits one of the lectures of Jean-Paul Sartre, something that has become a rare event these days. Twenty years ago he was the god of youth, and even today he loves especially to appear before young people, since for him the future has always been the authentic dimension of the human, and he despises the search for lost time just as much as the romantic eroticism of death. "Le faux, c'est la mort" (falsehood is death), he had written. His words address themselves not to those for whom the false already corrupts the look and roughens the voice, but to the young who still are what they promise to become, who stride toward what is coming, toward the event in world and space against which they measure their ego and for which they have to constitute it. Sartre is speaking to the students in the great hall of a large Western European university about the Russell Tribunal. A. had come less on account of the theme—about which he is adequately informed—than for the sake of the speaker himself. For many years, he has held him in great respect, developing thereby a strong intimacy, the one-sidedness of which he was scarcely conscious of. He had aged with Sartre. Only a shabby seven years separate him, the younger one, from his master, but seven years which, as the two of them, the philosopher and his reader-pupil, were climbing down the rungs of the ladder, had shrunk in scale to an inconsequential time-span so that A. could gradually feel he was the same age as the lecturer. He had seen him about twenty years ago. At that time, Sartre was youth personified and spoke not only into the future but quite rightly even in its name. He stood both at the beginning and at the peak of his fame; his existentialism was the last word in the history of ideas. That is only a little more than two decades ago. In 1946, in spite of his much discussed "ugliness," even described by Sartre himself in his autobiography, the philosopher exuded a strong physical force of attraction, something virile and powerful. But, my God, now he has become a frail, tired gentleman, a senile man with flaccid, pale-gray face, an emaciated body, and an exhausted, rattling voice; he has become old with time weighing inside of him, and for a few seconds A. finds it difficult to recognize again the Sartre from the springtime of 1946.

He is most deeply moved about something fundamentally simple and constantly known, but which again and again is totally new: that a human being can come to such a state. A. knows, as everyone knows, that the great philosopher in whose honor the students are now rising to their feet is quite sick, enough so that his biological age must be relatively higher than his chronological age and his physical decay therefore without exemplary value for the age of a sixty-three-year-old. But while the lecturer speaks, logically very rigorous as always, with the force of his own dialectically sharpened formulations, nailing the political developments down in brilliant points as he philosophically justifies the Russell Tribunal against the American Vietnam War, A., who is only listening absent-mindedly to the text of the lecture, grows aware that it is not nearly as much the philosopher's bodily fragility that shifts him into the psychological state of painful and resigned tenderness as it is Sartre's *social* age. Even the philosopher of breaking the limits of the self has become a prisoner—not of his fame and reputation, as the speaker who introduced the lecture said, since Sartre has just broken out of that—but instead the prisoner of the time stacked up inside him, still only speaking the texts of his role in life, still only being what he accomplished and therefore being conditioned by the society that struck the balance of his life and work and compels him to be no other than just Jean-Paul Sartre, who wrote certain books and not others, who in 1948 founded a political party that did not even become a sect, who refused the Nobel Prize, and who, as the philosopher who broke down boundaries, set his own limits, limits that at this stage can no longer be crossed, especially by a man who has already aged, who may live fifteen more years or just as easily only five.

The unfortunately somewhat rasping voice speaks, appeals, analyzes, exercises an undiminished highly sharpened intellect, gives orders. Two and a half thousand people hang on every word with extremely anxious attention. It is quite obvious that standing is not easy for the speaker. Periodically, he braces his hands very high against his hips as if to help his body carry its own weight. His hair, twenty years ago copper-colored and thick, is now steel-gray and scant and only covers his balding head in single strands. But A. is thinking that even that is not the essential thing, although it intensifies the painful tenderness he feels as though he were standing down there himself and had to support the weight of his own burdensome body with his arms braced against his hips. What touches him, more than the physical decline of the great man, even more than the knowledge that Sartre has to remain Sartre even as an aging man, even to promote the memory of Che Guevara without being able to become another Che Guevara, what makes him, A., feel the hardship of his own situation as an aging person is the insight into the way the two and a half thousand attentive and respectful young people are stealing from the old man down below the last years of his life—through the mere fact of their being young and going forth into a world that belongs to them and *only* them. They will read other books than those of Jean-Paul Sartre, other than those that Jean-Paul Sartre read. They will populate a world without Sartre: the anti-Sartre world, which will expand even as image, word, and deed of the, by then, already deceased Sartre will be as petrified and rigid as his gravestone. The future of these young people is set within them as a fact of their being young. In this context, that means that they are ready both to seize the world and to flow effusively into it. But since this future world without Sartre is within them, in their projects to do this and that, to write books, to mount platforms, to watch movies, and to go to the Congo, since they carry the anti-Sartre world within them, they are becoming themselves Sartre's adversaries. —Now they get up once again from their amphitheatrical benches and applaud. They cannot know that the esteem they display for the aged man who snatches up his papers and makes for the exit on his tiny feet is "dis-esteem" and a malicious condemnation. They would have to be old themselves to realize how the respect offered to that which *was* and *is* becomes disparagement: for the respectful view of what has been does not allow any longer the belief that the latter can still *become*. Their tribute is somber, like an obituary. In it they anticipate the philosopher's death. Applause. Bravo, bravo. But now to ourselves and the world! A good and great old man. After him greater and better ones are coming    and we, the young, will be there with them. —The gigantic hall empties.

On his way home through the cold city, whose new streets and buildings have changed so much that it's a daily effort for him to find his way and not drive into a one-way street, A. is alone. But he is mentally with Jean-Paul Sartre, whose social age is his, even though he is himself a shrinking seven years younger. Unlike his great comrade, who at this moment is probably retiring exhausted in his hotel room, he is not a famous philosopher. But he is also already what he was, and from him, too, the young people leaving the lecture and crossing the street have stolen the world that they are ready to make from his into theirs. They are pleasing to look at. They are a horror. One can, one must, instruct them. But for ever and ever, one must be ashamed in their presence, before their embraces, before the books they plan, the political parties they will establish. Just how simple it is: society ascribes a social age to us. It destroys us only when this social age has reached a level at which the world takes stock of what we have done or not done. At that point, society follows the unwritten laws of youth, developed anew every day, by human beings who have both the state of becoming and the future entirely to themselves. Our social extinction in age is already settled, regardless of whether our name is Sartre or X., regardless of whether we are accompanied by applause and the light of flashbulbs or drive through the streets anonymously. We are constituted as being such and such and having this and that—and thereby locked out of that which becomes. The future is already at an end. Our social ego has been given to us no matter how much we may be inclined in lonely hours to coddle a fictitious "true" one. If we can only still choose to be Talleyrand in the madhouse or the great painter in the Café du Dôme? But no.

We can just as easily reject both the acceptance of the verdict and its open refusal—as most try to do, giving their old age its appearance of ridiculously sunny good fortune. Then we withdraw into a self-deception that certainly never really takes us in: we are neither the negated nor the mentally ill, just aging and old people, anybody and everybody, lost in the indifference of normality. How are you? Fine, thanks, O.K. for my age, just right under the circumstances. And a false smile on the face of the person asking the question, a bashful one on the person questioned. That can be handled fairly easily; who'd want to deny it? The world, agreeably touched because it doesn't have to be scrupulous, talks of a positive attitude. That we age in dignity, as it's called, without revolt, without lament, is required—and such a demand made of us, in alliance with our own weakness and lassitude, eventually satisfies.

A positive attitude and dignified aging without complaint have two aspects. One can pursue change and, as a favorite prank of self-deception, "stay young with the young." Society with its economic institutions helps vigorously. Life begins at forty, at fifty. "How to retire happily at fifty-five in California." "Women can be sexually happy after menopause." Clothes make the man; if you wear them young, then you are young. The same society that annihilates the aging by putting them in the straitjacket of an unchangeable existence or even expels them from its economic process requires them to consume their age as they once consumed their youth. The temptation is great, for whoever gives in to it eventually really catches here and there a few small crumbs of the world: one carries himself young and fashionably, marries a young woman, and, while wheezing, dances the jerk at sixty; the other buzzes after time, possibly ahead of it, appears embarrassingly willing to be enchanted about the conquest of space, wayward kids, and the latest novels, things supposedly filling him with enthusiasm even though in truth he hankers after his peace and quiet and wants to read Fontane.[2] With this attitude, those who try to remain young in splendor do not find themselves in agreement with society, but no doubt in accord with its economic and publicistic facade. They do what is prescribed for them by advertisements, posters, popular newspaper articles, and even serious sociological investigations, formulated in their own way to serve the apparatus of society and published for its purposes. It seems to be very pleasant when one is permitted to obey. And it doesn't amount to anything when the command is given against the better judgment of the commander and one bows in obedience against one's own reasonable insight.

A "positive attitude" to aging can also have a completely different allure. This will certainly not be sanctioned by the economic apparatus, but through convention it has risen to an honor: we are speaking of the retreat of the aging into an idyll. Society's annihilation is not negated by them because they gasp for time but, on the contrary, because they affirm its rapid pace by withdrawing from it. It is attractive and good to age. I've been young and can also join in the conversation; I've gotten old, and thus what I say counts. Long since the aging have feathered their nests and are tenderly cultivating them with "Let, oh world, oh let me be."[3] They are satisfied that society grants them the peace of nothingness by letting them be what they are and were. It no longer expects much from them, only that they replay what's departed from this life and been declared dead—a profound relief. They say they are harvesting. They sit with a sunny visage at the window and take a look at the world as if through a reversed opera glass. Whatever races and struggles around in it is very small to their eyes. *Les jeux sont faits* (the chips are down): they don't need to play anymore and can shift to kibitzing and giving detached advice; they've done their part; now the others can show what they can do. Without envy they watch the others wear themselves out. Blessed time, I have already seen so much, thrones fall, countries arise, philosophies seize the world and fade after two decades, fashions come and go, people are born and die; you've got to stick to the great and eternal things and to the strongbox you can take with you. Old persons idyllically aging take as little notice of society's annihilation as those who stay young and animated: the latter convince themselves they can catch up with the time that rolls over them, the former simply deny it by setting their conceptual poem of eternity against it. Both live in untruth and a *mauvaise foi* (bad faith).

But those who try to live the truth of their condition as aging persons, though they dispense with the lie, don't escape the ambiguity that inevitably has to turn out in the end as an open contradiction. They accept an-nihilation, knowing that in this acceptance they can only preserve themselves if they rise up in revolt against it, but that their revolt—and here the acceptance is an affirmation of something irrevocable—is condemned to failure. They say no to an-nihilation and at the same time yes to it, for only in this futile denial can one present oneself at all *as oneself* to the inevitable. They do not lose themselves in the it's-all-the-same-to-me of a normalcy without self, nor do they look for refuge in the madhouse, nor do they deceive themselves with a mask of youth, nor with a deeply deceiving idyll of aging. They are as society prescribes: what they are, a nothing, and yet in the recognition of being nothing still something. They make their negation in the look of the others into something of their own and rise up against it. They embark on an enterprise that cannot be accomplished. That is their chance and is, perhaps, the only possibility they have of truly aging with dignity.

# Not to Understand the World Anymore

Whoever gets to the threshold, one earlier in years, the other a little later, some armored with honesty, others snared in self-deception, all of them turning out to be less solid, they all have to learn at a certain point that they do not understand the world any more. This aspect of social aging—getting *culturally* old in the widest sense—usually becomes clear in a rather slow, undramatic process of successive insights. At first there is often only a numb feeling of aversion against what a particular aging person might call the "cultural jargon" of his epoch. With this feeling, he cuts himself off from asking whether he doesn't also speak such a jargon, albeit superannuated, and not, as he thinks, a pure language, *the* language plain and simple. Then slight discomfort accompanies him while reading certain periodicals and books, and he will be inclined to talk with a disapproving, resigned shrug of the shoulders about fashion, snobbism, isms, verbal pomposity, talk he often denies himself, since no one likes to stand off in backward spitefulness. This thoroughly trivial resistance against the new and unusual may be recognized by those educated in the history of ideas as a constantly recurring phenomenon. They may know what transpired in Paris at the first exhibition of the impressionists in 1874, why it had to happen as it did, on what basis the resistance against Monet and his friends eventually grew lame in embarrassment.

But today, it will still not be easy for them to convert their displeasure with lettrism (or infra- and ultra-lettrism)[1] into a demonstration of tolerance—for them only a form of incomprehension anyway. The insubordination of the aging confines itself here not only to those cultural phenomena that require an expenditure of intellectual effort, a readjustment of one's sensibility, but to the most incidental developments, such as clothing fashions.

No matter how often A. leafs through the fashion magazines, knowing precisely that she will have her clothes prepared with a moderate downplaying of fashionable requirements, the new models are a pronounced displeasure to her and seem to be absurd. This time, too, A. is disagreeably stirred by what is to her the blatantly idiotic extravagance of the models. As she has already done sometimes on similar occasions, she gets out her photo album with its old pictures in order to find once again what she thinks was really attractive and becoming in contrast to the irritating creations the designers are burdening her with this year. But with her first look at the little pictures from the late thirties, something happens that she had already anticipated even before she got out the album, something she had still denied even in the midst of her foreboding and against a better judgment based on past experiences: right before her eyes, the fashion of her youth, *her* fashion, an essential part of the ego built up by her memory, becomes something completely impossible, at least as grotesque as the models with whom she will have to make friends in the coming season. There she is herself, standing under a tree. Supple waves of hair regularly undulating into her cheeks, a skirt reaching almost to her ankles, a jacket with comically cut concave padded shoulders, an indescribable slouch hat, eyes turned up in a way that, shaking her head, she cannot describe as anything but audacious. How could she and even the others ever have liked anything like that? Furthermore, she has to learn how even the most banal consequences of events never turn out simply. If it were solely what people say and talk about without thinking—old-fashioned things are funny and embarrassing because they have been known for a long time and we were there when they were overtaken by time, in contrast to the historic things, unknown for a long time, at whose sad capitulation we were not present—if things really behaved that way, we could not explain how the outmoded immediately loses any ridiculousness when it is no longer merely looked at but *remembered*. A. claps the photo album shut, closes her eyes, sinks into the past: she has tracked down the little hat, padded jacket, ankle-length skirt and ferreted them out as her own; now she reconstructs the gesture of turned up eyes and is again totally certain of its charming effect. Those former waves of hair falling into her cheeks, now, since A. thinks she can touch them again with her hands, have regained their grace of 1938. The lesion has healed over. A. may once again trust the antipathy she felt for the new model and had to give up in embarrassment when she looked at the old photos. Of course, she will recommend the fashionable creations to her dressmaker as an inspiration, but she will wear these clothes against her own conviction as an unfortunately necessary concession to society. She herself will remain the girl of that time, beyond such up-to-date costumes—and will protect herself from the pictures that question her self-esteem: these show her the fashion of that time, broken, corrupted, transformed by the look of today; the wardrobe of yesterday regains its authenticity in *memory*. The unreality of an event that cannot be translated from the objective physicality of the cerebral process into the subjective existence of a remembering perception is more real than the tangible reality of a picture.

That conclusion still has not expressed anything about the cultural alienation of aging human beings, about the stubborn indignation, welling up inside them against their better judgment, at all that is new coming toward them. But maybe it signals that a start has been made. We can abstract from A.'s experience, this thoroughly banal experience that each and every aging person can reproduce at will, and shift to the basic facts that are hidden in it. When she leafs through the photo album, A. sees the fashion of the past from within the sign system of the present, where she anxiously remains in spite of her resistance. In her process of remembering, she relates the same data about fashion to the sign system of former times, to which she is likewise bound, having nonetheless constructed her ego out of her reminiscences.

The cultural alienation of the aging person cannot be interpreted except as the difficulty of finding one's way in an unknown array of signs, even among completely new signals. Just as an auto driver who was traveling through England for the first time before the traffic signals had been thoroughly coordinated with those on the continent lost all self-confidence and was only able to continue slowly, with a feeling of constriction, the aging err through the cultural signs of their epoch. For A., whenever she feels distressed by the latest fashion, the half-exposed upper thigh of a woman always has the significance it had in her youth: a provocative acknowledgment of erotic readiness and consequently—again according to the sign syntax of the past—indecency. In the system of the present, however, the signs have been arranged differently. The naked upper thigh is not an acknowledgment of erotic readiness any more; it is no longer a provocation; and provocation can no longer be assigned to the concept of indecency. As it happens, what we specifically call the meaning of a sign is perhaps not unconditionally the signified itself but instead the relationship of one sign to others, so that the meaningful system consists in the relations of each single sign to every other one.

To the extent that the aging try to situate the cultural phenomena of this current time to accord with the reference points of their past—which was *their* time because it promised them the future, the world, and space—they become more and more strangers to their epoch. The strangeness becomes manifest to them as uncertainty, and it objectifies itself in ill humor and impotent rejection. A sixty-year-old man who follows the intellectual discussion of the day will frequently tend to view the conflict between rationalism and irrationalism, the Bergson-Benda argument, as the cardinal question dividing the intellectual leaders. If he then becomes aware that the Marxists, whom he has considered not without justification to be at least the arms-bearers of the rationalistic forces, are now partly declaring allegiance to Heidegger, the intellectual spirit of the age will necessarily seem out of place to him, even literally out of its mind: the philosophical mathematics of his epoch is turning into a witch's one-times-one.[2] The same fear, even panic, seizes him when the flashback in a contemporary movie does not have any significant temporal logic and, in the midst of the new order of signs, he is not only unable to continue to evaluate the film aesthetically but must take the greatest effort just to follow the action—which in the sense of an earlier sign syntax is in many ways no such thing any more. Just as the aging cannot find their way in a city that changes its topography from year to year, from month to month, just as their world atlas is of no use to them anymore since the former British and

French colonies have long since become new self-sufficient states whose names they can only retain with difficulty, so they wander desperately through the underbrush of new tone series in music— it makes no difference whether instrumental or concrete—and new structures of words and sentences. One has to have patience with them, as much with their reactionary and obdurate lack of understanding in the face of new poetic structures as with their tolerance, conditioned by the same nonunderstanding, and their precipitous, but illegitimate, affirmation of everything the day brings them.

Here above all we need to bear in mind that within our contemporary world the sign systems are extremely differentiated. A supersystem is no doubt constantly establishing itself as the result of a complicated process by which importance is distributed. In our days, this supersystem ranks structuralism, for instance, ahead of existentialism; the New Novel, independent of chronology and no longer obligated to the delineation of character, ahead of the realistic one; the Marxism of a Marcuse, drawn especially from Hegel, as more progressive than that of the Kantian Max Adler. Even concepts like "Papa's cinema" have already made their way into the daily press; the aging themselves use them and thereby accept the value system contained in them, even if with mistrust and discomfort. Within each prevailing supersystem, partly in contradiction to it, but never completely independent of it, special systems are formed. These special systems, unstable arrangements of taste in the aesthetic realm, no less slack and unclear intellectual schemata in the rational-intellectual realm, overlap each other. Anyone who lives mentally within the system of neopositivism conforms to points of orientation different from those of the structuralist, while the latter is related to different references, different not only from those of the former, but also from those of a Marxist, an existentialist, or a phenomenologist. But common to them is their independence from outmoded systems: what was called the philosophy of life around the turn of the century is foreign and a matter of indifference to them; in this respect they all move within the complex of their epoch. The more encompassing a system is, the more it is both abstract and undifferentiated for the subject. The supersystem or the systems of the epoch have a less immediate grip on the individual than the narrower structural disposition in which each lives. The concepts of the philosophy they've selected concern the structuralists more than those of Marxism, but in common with the Marxists they have an easier access to the structural disposition of Marxism than to that of a Theodor Lessing or a Ludwig Klages.[3] The narrowest and most concrete system is naturally always the individual one whose center is then no longer the "spirit of the times," nor even this or that doctrine, but the *individuals* themselves in their own person: here then the references become psychological data. If they appear as emotionally colored, they have existential density.

Because every individual is the center of a specific sign system, because the middle reference point of the system is his or her own existence and has arranged all other points of reference as they are and not otherwise, it is therefore so extraordinarily difficult for the aging to grasp the signs of an age which, coming into being right before their eyes, is steadily ceasing to be at their disposal. It might be difficult, for example, for a man getting on in years to declare anything like Ulrich's conversations with his friend Walter in *The Man without Qualities,* the *operationes spirituales* of Mssrs. Naphta and Settembrini in *The Magic Mountain,* or the anticlericalism of the title character in Martin du Gard's *Jean Barois* as insignificant or just historically interesting. Or he'll have the same experience as A. observing her old photos: he might smile over the arguments carried on by the Jewish Jesuit and the Italian Freemason in the thin air of Davos, but when he switches directly to them after reading a modern dialectician, he will, just like A. with the fashion of 1938, as soon as he has pushed his dialectician away even for a minute, *experience them as he remembers them,* as *the* still essential discussions, and will finally deem today's dialectical wit to be superfluously overprofound or high-hatted babbling. For the narrowest of systems is that particular one which, giving power and making order, is the middle point of one's ego, the constituent of this ego: every relation, every figure of this system is a piece of oneself. If it is now the case that for the aging the supersystem of their epoch and the majority of the infrasystems formed within the super-system still only contain greatly transformed elements of their personal system, their alienation will be total and the ways out remaining to them will only lead into still deeper alienations. If they answer the given system with a curt refusal—"Ah, yes, all that calls itself philosophy these days is empty talk, hopeless drivel is offered us as painting, anarchical quackery presented as poetry"— then they step out of their time, become strangers to the world and downright cranks. If they try, however, to accept the new systems, for which they must always pay the price of the demo-lition of their individual system, they then forego what was yester-day still their own, become (in the exact meaning of the word) inauthentic, and cannot with this dubious business even bargain for the recognition of the representatives of the prevailing system. Quite rightly the latter will say that, to be sure, such old people mean very well and, though old, are at least always "receptive to new ideas," but necessarily lack the right understanding. With that remark it all falls into place. The new signs and their relationships always have full validity and accessibility only for those who are themselves a part of their invention and design; they are only learned while being created. The strangers who are guests of former times will constantly find their way around in them only with difficulty, like the driver of a car in the midst of unknown traffic signs.

For a long time, A. has been trying to keep up with a clever and vehement modern literary critic who without much ado has declared one of the favorite writers of his youth, the Swiss writer born in Swabia, Hermann Hesse, to be a producer of kitsch. O.K., even he, A., has not remained unconditionally faithful to poor Hesse, and now if he were to reread the part where Demian and his Romantic friend Pistorius stare together into the glowing coals, even he would probably find it tedious reading. Peter Caminzind's love for the little bourgeois daughter Rösi Girtanner strikes him as rather narrow and stodgy. If he happens to open *Steppenwolf* again and read about the passion of Harry Haller, the Steppenwolf, for his androgynous Hermine, A. admits there is definitely something both pompous and comic about it. For God's sake, an old fellow of fifty has belatedly learned that it is OK to sleep with an attractive woman! Hesse should not have made such a fuss about the trivial story. But to deal with the word kitsch as briskly as the critic does seems to A. to be a somewhat risky business. He'd like both to pull himself together to a modern critical vehemence and to recommend to the critic the kind of tolerance for the old writer that he himself is ready to offer the new, knowing in the process that tolerance in that place is not exactly tolerance and that the new is always right quite simply because it is further along in time. How does it all relate to kitsch and cultural aging, A. asks himself. Does it happen in this case the way it does with fashion, where yesterday's style is em-

barrassing and ridiculous and a painful shame solely for the
thoroughly sufficient reason that it is unfortunately yesterday's
style? Apparently. In any case, it is striking how both in fashion
and in literary aesthetics the historical—and even when it was
not sanctified by traditional education—does not succumb to the
process: baroque writers like Lohenstein and Hofmannswaldau
are curious, but no less ridiculous than the peacock-like men's
fashions of the Renaissance. Laughter and ashamed distress,
therefore kitsch—A. is thinking how that is constantly what was
*experienced yesterday* as something *fashionable*. Hesse and the adjective "comely,"[4] they've had it now because they belong to
yesterday and were popular yesterday, that is, they were worn
out by mass use, devalued. Kafka, who was writing his cold
pieces of horror at the same time Hesse gave himself over to
comeliness, was not caught by the kitsch-making process, a historical process, even where it has to do with contemporary
kitsch. That's not because his work is constructed of elements
that are so very different from those of Hesse—by the way, are
they really very different, and is it pure coincidence that precisely
Hesse was one of the first to refer to Kafka with emphasis?—but
because the man from Prague, contrary to the Swabian Swiss,
had never been a contemporary fashion. There was only a Kafka
fashion when Kafka no longer existed; it therefore could make its
appearance with the allure of an antifashion, constituting itself as
both historic and pointing toward the future.

No matter how hard he tries, A. finds nothing more than a
theoretical and purely abstract relief in trying to remember how
aesthetic and intellectual transformations have run their course
or in trying to legitimize historically his cultural outmodedness.
For he is outmoded in an incurable way, since he understands
the kitsch of the word "comely" with his head but not with his

senses. Thus he does not at first doubt that his critical mind has found itself on wild goose chases, because he never took the trouble to question the relationships "comely" might have had to the other signs within the sign system in which Hesse was living. How did the incriminating adjective's lines of reference connect to the single aesthetic components of the everyday language of the time, to the fashions in dress, to the language of poetry in the school readers, and to the other language that was at that time "modern," to the current sound and image structures? The young girls à la Rösi Girtanner played Sinding's "Rustle of Spring" on the piano. Liliencron was read. Storm had not yet been dead for long. Comely was not yet comely, Hesse was not Hesse any more than the Hölderlin of 1800 had been Hölderlin.[5] —A. is thinking how his energetic critic did not consider such things when sternly passing judgment, rightly or wrongly, about signs that had meaning only within a class of signs. However, the critical judge of Hesse cannot be disposed of so easily: he has made use of his competence as a man of his time to build on the sign system of his time along with others and has placed the Hesse signs into new relationships, thereby revaluing and changing them. The critic's action was not illicit, for the systems are certainly not static but are in a process of permanent renewal. "Comely" and Hesse, Hölderlin and the walls that stand speechless in the wind, even Dehmel and his *djagloni gleia klirrla*,[6] it all goes from one year to another into a new sign system and changes its meaning. This critic has acted as a steward of signs and the giver or the taker of meaning. One has to let him do as he likes.

As the case may be. A. is not asked at all whether he consents to a procedure or not. His deliberations, the thought sequences of an aging person, break apart on a threshold of thinking where he must recognize that he himself *can never be right in opposition to that sharp critic,* even if the latter is not always thoroughly right about everything. That's because for A. there is a special inextinguishable state of affairs regarding outmoded phenomena: these phenomena are signs within his individual sign system. Their referential links are tied not only to intersubjectively fixable reference points—thus "comely" does not exclusively belong to the girls playing Sinding's "Rustle of Spring" or to the essays in the *Neue Rundschau* at that time—but to definite, highly personal circumstances, to apartments, streets, cities he lived in when he read of comeliness and *djagloni,* girls he loved, of course, but much more trifling things as well: suits he wore, cafés he frequented. It is simply impossible for him—or anyone else—to break out of the individual system whose vital aroma he has dragged with him through the years. A. suddenly has some understanding for the former avant-gardist Ernest Ansermet who wrote a totally reactionary book against serial music. He grasps the humiliating scene he witnessed, where the former rebel, Oskar Kokoschka, now grown old, poured forth veritable enormities about modern painting. It is no more possible for him, much younger than Kokoschka and Ansermet, to get away from "comeliness," i.e., to arrange this "comeliness" in a new class of signs—because, as signs of his individual system, they still have grown into his person—than for the great conductor and the painter to believe that their vanguard of 1910 had not conquered the last impassable terrain.

It is true, he can learn new signs, he tells himself, if he makes the effort, and he can then get a general idea of today's sign systems, even if not all of them. Poetry, for example: he can't stop reading Liliencron, whom he had loved at sixteen, or Rilke, whom he read somewhat later, or Heym, Trakl, Werfel, Ehrenstein, who followed them and became elements of his individual system. Everything goes on and will continue going on. But there in front of him is a poem. "hin the beginning was the word hand the word was with / god hand god was the word hand the word his become flesh / hand has dwelled hamong hus . . ." which after a few bewildering variants then ends with the lines ". . . shin she sheginning shas the word hand she word / shas shith shod shand flod was the word shand / she ford shis shecome shlesh shand / shas shwelled shamong shus." All right. It's not wicked, nor atrocious; it is also not at all so new-fangled that one holds one's head in blaring perplexity. On A.'s face there are no petty bourgeois sneers, nor expressions of conservative indignation. Here and there he has read theoretical writings that made the syntax of such signs at least half-way clear to him. He is full of honorable effort. But the labor of love is in vain and he cannot get himself to like it—ah, where has *djagloni* gone?—away with "shamong shus." And all at once the uncanny fact is illuminated to him that for the aging, not only their body—which transforms itself from something carried into something weighing them down, a load—but even their culture, like an insufficient heart, a sensitive stomach, a weak jaw, becomes toil and trouble.

It is extremely distressing when new signs and systems have to be learned every day. Between 1945 and 1948, it was not so very easy to decipher the intellectual map of French existentialism. No sooner was A. sure of its information than he had to hear that its topoi were no longer recognized, that new border lines were being drawn. Lacan, Foucault, Althusser were busy inventing sign systems and enacting codices, which A. had to declare himself incapable of translating into Sartre-signs. It is a great drudgery for someone who speaks the language of Proust to learn anew that of Le Clézio. If he tries to make the effort and decides on the study of aesthetic writings, he'll probably more or less manage with "she ford shis shlesh." Then, when he sees that sort of thing, he'll raise his hat with a feeling of dejected respect and the consciousness of his own outmodedness. But it's better if it's settled when he doesn't see it. Like the mountain he can no longer climb and which is therefore the negation of his person, the sign language of modern culture presents itself to him as the denial of his ego: he can then certainly say to himself that the nay-sayers are right about him just as the Romanticists were right, right in the course of time about the discontented old Goethe, but he cannot enjoy the destruction of his individuality that runs parallel to the demolition of his sign system. He has to repudiate what the passage of time—whether called progress or not is not the issue—has disposed of, pushed into the grave. He doesn't feel like coming to the happy wake.

And just as his comrade in aging sets aside her photo album, closes her eyes, and is able to see in the process of remembering the deceased signs of fashion functioning attractively again in the entire sign system of yesterday, A. recites to himself the lines of Dehmel no one wants to hear anymore. And with a bad conscience to boot, because he knows that it's no longer possible to make much of *djagloni*. In addition, he has the somewhat sorrowful feeling that he's acting like the old fool who hums with dewy eyes the hit songs of his youth.

The cultural existence of human beings is a form of their social existence. What applies to their extended social being consequently has the force of law for all possibilities of culture as well. At a certain moment—or better, an uncertain one—appearing from case to case according to a person's particular relationships, each can only become what he or she already is. The chances of transcending oneself culturally are long over with. The quantity of formative elements already accumulated and defining consciousness is so large that it takes on the quality of immobility. Just as the body in aging always becomes more and more mass and less and less energy, the spirit, here understood as cultural receptor, behaves likewise, becoming ponderous and heavy, with itself and with time, so that in its increasing sluggishness it no longer is inclined to stir when new signs challenge it.

At what age does this adversity befall a human being? Is it a destiny of everyone? Are there not perhaps people whose systems, assumed or even created mostly in their youth or at the latest in their middle years, are so *in advance* of temporarily valid systems that in aging and in old age they have in particular circumstances the tremendous gratification of watching the spectacle of the "spirit of the age" lazily crawling after them until all at once the cultural majority ratified their system, meaning that for them the whole problem has not existed at all? In answer to the first question, probably no one can supply any information. Cultural aging, the decline of the power of receptivity and the will to receive, the weariness and resignation in the face of the demands of every new day—they are just as individual as the physiological aging process. Perhaps the age of fifty marks the point where one turns the corner, but that is only a vague estimate, for reliable statistical material is not available. However, the second question can be answered, even right away. It's true, no one can say, "I am ahead of my time." No one knows what's avant-garde; only what *was* avant-garde can be determined. Yet many creative individuals have been both satisfied and soothed in being able to say they have left their time behind them. As an aging old man, Arnold Schoenberg experienced that the system crucial for him, twelve-tone music, became the dominating one. Most of the great painters since impressionism, whose pictorial ordering structure and laws were reviled when they were young, experienced the triumph of these systems. That does not exclude, first, that in certain circumstances during their lifetime their temporarily victorious central systems were overtaken and superseded by others and, second, that in the sphere of separate systems they might have felt in their middle years already culturally aged. A great musician, constantly in advance of his musical era, can also be mentally indolent and behind the times with respect to the art of cinematography. A poet who creates a new sign system can simultaneously have arch-conservative tastes in the fine arts. The difficulty of theoretically capturing cultural aging, the cultural alienation of aging, and the denial of the world by not understanding the world, even in only partially valid propositions, is connected with the mutability and incomprehensibility of what has been called here a system. The prevailing supersystem—which we can also talk about in an older linguistic custom as the spirit of the age or the spirit of the era— does it have to be taken back as a concept? No and yes. No: because quite obviously such a system exists as long as one at least watches the intellectual contours of an age from a certain distance and with a superficiality sufficient to one's daily cultural life. If we accept the present as this year of 1968, when these words are being written down, then a number of reference points will be recognized with lines connected to the outline of the spirit of the era. New Criticism, new cinema, experimental poetry, theater of the absurd, pop art, happenings, and whatever may flash into one's mind with a sudden flare or like a slogan—it will all appear as a *Gestalt*, as a unit held together by something more than a few dates of the year, no matter how contradictory such single phenomena may appear to others. Nevertheless, the concept of the supersystem must be withdrawn when the look is no longer a fleeting one, for then the factual situations lose everything that makes them a totality. The spirit of the age or the supersystem becomes a number of single systems, a quantity without gestalt. Then even the concept of cultural simultaneity is no use to anyone, for in the end it really reduces itself to the abstract fact of mere chronology. A society of the friends of André Gide carries out its intellectual social game within Gide's sign system and does not concern itself with the avant-garde group of young authors who circle around the periodical *Tel quel*. The Anglo-Saxon neopositivists keep constructing indefatigably the articulation of their organizing principles and do not take cognizance of the fact that there are movements like Neomarxism and structuralism. For the friends of concrete music the twelve-tone system has already been discarded. Serial composers maintain that concrete music is heading for a dead end.

The contradictory fact that there is a prevailing supersystem—regardless of whether it exists only for the conservative who rejects abstract and neorealistic painting, serial and concrete music, neopositive and structuralistic analyses, amalgamating them all together as newfangled humbug—the fact therefore that such a thing as the spirit of the age both exists and does not exist can at first seem trivial: to be sure, there is also the forest and there are various regions of this forest and finally the individual trees. Still, in our context of social aging, this in itself banal contradiction, which can be resolved by taking the supersystem, infrasystem, and eventually individual phenomena as possible hypotheses in describing reality, becomes an existential problem well beyond the categories of the trivial and relevant. Culturally aging human beings find themselves, in any case, in a foreign, enigmatic world even when they are free of conservative arrogance, that faint-heartedness of those who've gone to the dogs. It is for each of them of little consequence that the prevailing supersystem, whatever it may be, is composed of a complex of partly different and diverging infrasystems, that there is in truth no cultural simultaneity, that all systems also contain elements of one's own systems, that possibly on a day coming after one has gone, components of one's systems will magnificently rise again in modified form. What concerns the culturally aging and what strikes to their core is the denial that the epoch giving birth to itself holds up against their individual system every day. And this revocation that they read out of every newspaper article, find confirmed in every exhibition of modern art, that is implicitly expressed in most of the new books that appear in the book market—it makes itself known in our days in an especially injurious form.

The density of the amount of information available requires that every new sign system, once it has barely come into being, take the liberty of addressing a broad public in radical abbreviation so that it may democratize itself in a perverse way by cutting itself down to slogan units and thereby penetrating into the most insignificant conversations. No matter how hard they may try, the culturally aging will never succeed in "being in." For example, one of them has just read, not without a good will that he successfully and with considerable zeal wrenched from his reluctance, a book by the philosopher of popular culture, Marshall McLuhan, and has tried to formulate a few thoughts about it for himself, when he hears a secondary-school teacher next to him saying, "The medium is the message." Not only is his individual sign system invalidated by that remark, but his effort and his good will are made ridiculous. It is no comfort to him that the secondary teacher, having picked up the slogan somewhere in an article in a popular magazine, has let this thoughtless cud-chewing diminish the value of this fashionable philosophy and thereby apparently confirmed his own poor assessment of this series of thoughts. On the contrary. Our aging person has to sit back and watch as the processes of formation, popularization, and devaluation roll off at an increasingly rapid tempo. That discourages him thoroughly, not only because it explains to him in the most radical way the futility of the tiresome work he put into learning about this subject, but because he is realizing that between the dynamic supersystem, impossible to overtake and every hour displaying different features—i.e., the spirit of the age—and his individual system, developed over decades from basic elements, even greater numbers of systems are inserting themselves, all with the effect that his own system constantly moves further away until he scarcely recognizes it anymore. For him the logical question whether the acceleration should be called progress is not even under discussion. Since he doesn't withdraw to the definitely unassailable but hopeless position of the intransigent conservative for whom cultural events once and for all found their climax and end point in his individual system with everything coming after only delusion and fool's play, he has to recognize the acceleration as an authentic phenomenon, unless he wants to be a stupidly proud nay-sayer from another world. He even has to incorporate what he tries to call fashion and snobbism into the authenticity of the acceleration and eventually consider the McLuhanite secondary teacher, whom he was ready to dismiss even yesterday as a gabby upstart, to be an awakened young man. Nothing new will seem to him as bizarre or as insignificant as the fact that the young man does not even give him credit for his consideration and won't have to accept it with respect. And with every new concession made to the spirit of the age a piece of his world falls in ruins like the still generally solid *Hôtels de Maître* on the boulevard that are being pulled down in order to erect in their place apartment houses with walls that are too thin.

Just as the fifty-year-old woman uses the new patterns to place her orders with her seamstress even though during the late afternoon hours she prefers to close her eyes and reexperience the jacket and hat of thirty years ago as a becoming piece of clothing, this culturally aging man keeps step. But the happenings of today suit him no more than the fashions of today suit her.

The consciousness of being outmoded, if it does not rigidify into a defensive posture denying the epoch, can be extraordinarily tormenting, thoroughly comparable to a persistent bodily pain. The stretch of time in which we move is unkind to the aging person, apparently more unkind than any past one was. The essential parts of every cultural individual system are formed in one's youth, due to the statistical curve of vitality and sensibility. If the individual system is now overpowered by a supersystem, constantly renewing itself with incessantly dynamic energy, and if the supersystem makes its appearance with all the ostentation conferred by the resources of modern information, then the aging, smothered by a contemporary culture defined as burden, suffer a loss of ego and world never to be replaced by anything or through any means. The fact that the respective prevailing supersystems, flowing over into each other, let those structural arrangements of order subsist, even when called in an educational sense "historical," i.e., when they are sanctioned and carried on as tradition through education, does not make the situation meaningful. That's because, whatever the handed-down and assumed educational values are, they usually have a very slight meaning within individual systems, regardless of whether the individual concerned has a historical educational profession or is a language professor, a teacher of history, an art historian, or the like. For those who have not specialized in older educational complexes and professionally concentrated cultural matters, the individual system is defined through signs that in their youth and possibly on into the years of the prime of life have been valid as modern. The individual system of a fifty-year-old educated person today is not specifically impregnated by Homer but by Kafka, not by Kant but by Husserl, by Nolde rather than by Tintoretto. Every supersystem integrates more or less happily the historical systems. Every one destroys those of yesterday and the time before yesterday and therefore precisely those to which the individual systems of aging persons had yielded themselves in countless varieties.

A., after having read himself weary with a number of modern articles from periodicals of philosophical, sociological, and meta-linguistic contents, is taking a rest from the effort. He then takes several volumes of an older provenance from his bookshelf to pull himself together and to find himself once again in them. He slams the books shut again; they are no match for the apparently insidiously clever essays he has worked through in desperate determination and furnished with marginal notes he knows are outspoken. No more than he could take a proudly beautiful girlfriend away from a twenty-five-year-old young man, no more than he could succeed in overtaking a man of thirty years in skiing, no matter how certain he may have once stood on his skis, can he triumph now over Philippe Sollers by reading Julien Green again. It's over, he has to tell himself, it's over and will never return again: the day I opened *Adrienne Mesurat* and took from this book the last word of modern novel writing. Gone forever, the moment in which I myself wrote that it is no longer possible, after the experiment of *Ulysses*, to conceive another novel. For around thirty years, I have lived an intellectually conscious life, and today, if I don't want to act like my seventy-year-old friend who, regardless of whether the opportunity is appropriate or not, pulls out a volume of Hölderlin and says, "*That's* what I read and it's enough for me!"—today, I have to confess to myself that for thirty years I have only exchanged one error for another. The self-evident truth that everything passes away because something new always appears on the horizon, the very old wisdom that one cannot step into the same river twice, is obvious only if one risks the impossible venture of stepping out of the space of what's been lived. Into what? Into a world without signs and systems, an empty world, an anti-universe. Then I perhaps can say to myself that it wasn't errors that followed each other in the series of years when I set up my cosmos, my system, from Dehmel and Rilke and Benn and Green and Proust and Joyce, but just stages. And with my proclamation of the end of the art of the novel in the post-Joyce era I was just as right as Sollers and his friends are right today with their novels, and I will be just as wrong as they tomorrow. Stages: of what? Of a development. Which is to lead where? Whoever does not know an answer to that question cannot legitimately speak of stages and may therefore only enumerate events. I sense that I want to give in either to a temptation that is just as dangerous as a defensive paralysis, in opposition to time, or to its opposite, the rash, imploring acceptance of everything the day brings me. I feel that I want to view my series of errors *sub specie aeternitas* along with the entire history of ideas known to me, which is no better or worse than not viewing at all. Eternity looks like the North Sea on calm but misty days when the sea and the dim sky blend into each other without a horizon. What I relate to the signless eternity, gray like the sea, I relate to nothing, and what is related to nothing is itself annihilated in the act of this not relating. Viewing cultural events from the point of view of eternity has a certain satisfaction for the culturally aging, but is also the saddest of all self-deceptions. The truth is, A. says to himself, not without a slight feeling of dizziness, that one cannot reasonably stand against time and not be permitted to chase after it, that one also does not have the alternative of removing oneself from the flow of time and holding to an eternal something that is a nothing. "Shad shamong shus" as well as *djagloni* and Gryphius[7] and God knows what else. One system like any other, worth just as much and just as little: whoever says this can just as easily be silent.

I may try to find comfort by whispering to myself how anything that now seems to fall to the destruction of time is still preserved by just this same time. What was fulfilling and held me together for a few decades, from Dehmel to Benn, from Hesse to Proust, from Cézanne to Francis Bacon, fulfilled the demand of those days belonging to me and was still pulled on by the wheel of time, even as it was being run over: nothing is ever completely lost. Comfort, a play of the mind. The notion of preservation in destruction is a construction of the philosophy of history without any significance in the field of the existential. To ferret out the passages where traces of Proust run through the work of Nathalie Sarraute is an occupation for literary historians. *My* Proust, whom I read for the first time in a definite time span, in a space connected only for me with this author, enclosed in a fragrance of being only still to be roused by my own memory—I cannot find it again in the books of Madame Sarraute. As a part of my existence it has been overtaken and left behind by this writer. What remains for me to do? I can try to catch up with myself by taking up Sarraute and with that involvement break the pact of life I once made with Proust. I can accomplish the same bailing-out operation by revoking my cultural contract—which is also a tie to myself—with my overtaken friends X Y Z. I distance myself from François Mauriac, whose fir-tree landscapes and torpid wine patricians belong to me, in hopes of getting to his son Claude.

But I will not arrive at the appointed place: Claude Mauriac belongs to a club that will not accept me. He is or wants to be a writer of tomorrow; thus he belongs to those who will still be there tomorrow, like the music-mathematician Iannis Xenakis, who composes with thinking machines. But tomorrow—that can mean: in ten minutes, in a year, in ten years, certainly at the latest in one and a half decades—I will no longer be there. It does not make any sense for me to break the fetters that chain me to the old Mauriac. The freedom from him that I would thereby gain isn't good for anything. To remain chained is a disgraceful resignation. To jump into the no longer inhabitable empty space of a freedom that is canceling itself out is only an act of panic. And no longer to feel chains as chains and freedom as freedom, to establish oneself in the mist of a North Sea eternity, where the former are nothing special and the latter can no longer be experienced—what then?

Well, it's clear: death. Cultural aging, for which there is more of a remedy than for physical decay, brings totally bad tidings, the annunciation of the end. Every withering away of a cultural sign system is death or the symbol of death. The imperative to die is witnessed by the aging. But right after it an imperative to become emerges, completely without them. Gloomy guests on the dark earth,[8] they hear the hoof beat, hear the trot. And as they fix themselves to life, they seize in deepest horror the past, forfeited, used-up systems that once were their life and therefore still are. Except that this life, encompassing the contradiction of human existence, surrounded by death, directed on toward death and only receiving its sense from death, has the oppressively paradoxical characteristic of being dead. The life of the aging, which we have called memory linked to time in another place and have set over against the young existence, which promises world and space, is, as far as its cultural benefits are concerned, nothing more than a cadaver. Comely Hesse, Dehmel singing his drinking songs, doubt-plagued François Mauriac, while one aging person still thinks he is creating from them the energies of his existence, they have already been and are in a state of putrefaction.

The dignity of cultural aging, entirely like that of the social aging in which it is embedded, can in turn only realize itself in the inconsistent revolt of fighting out a contradiction. The new systems exist. The aging must be ready to decipher them every day, without hope, on to the end. They cannot abandon their decomposing arrangements of order if they are not to abandon their egos; knowing the sinister necrophilia of their intellectual behavior, they have to preserve a worthless fidelity to those egos. That means: even here, in a hopeless venture of self-transcendence, having both to accept and to refuse their annihilation.

They do not understand the world any more;[9] the world they understand no longer exists. The compulsion to understand what cannot be understood leaves them little more than confinement to the past. They are not heroes, just whoever they may be: just as heroic as every "whoever" that ages and will die.

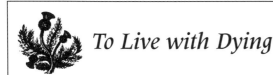

# To Live with Dying

Illnesses make their appearance. The face of the family doctor assumes now and then the features of professional worry, refined by clinical optimism. Companions born when you were born pass away. Statistics promise fifteen more years. The aging think of death. They think about it first as an objective event, in the categories of survivors. They wish everything to come to pass with a good ending. The family, just insofar as it's possible, is to be provided for, the burial is to take place in this or that form; consequently a last will is put down in writing. Once these conditions of order, required by convention and survivors, are established, those afflicted with aging come to themselves.

They are concerned that they won't be here in an all-too-foreseeable time (the last two decades went by in a frantic hurry for someone looking back at them!), and they feel urged to meditations on death. Right away, they will gain the experience that such reflection will not only result in nothing—after all, they've always known that—but that it's impossible. As the philosopher Vladimir Jankélévitch has written in his discomforting book *La*

*Mort*, to think of death is *penser l'impensable*, to think the un-thinkable. There is utterly nothing to think about death; genius and simpleton are equally thwarted in confronting this subject. Death is nothing, a nothing, a negativity. Thoughts about it are compromised to the most infinitesimal degree, even if, in accord with the law of compression, they are probably extremely dense. But are they thoughts? Hard to say. For anyone who ventures into thinking the unthinkable, words at least remain; we can call them thoughts just as well as not. Even the words shrink to something very small. Thinking of death becomes a monotonous and manic litany, undeniably similar to certain products of modern poetry: "I will die die will I die I will will I die die I will I will die." Or in French: "Je vais mourir mourir je vais je vais mou-rir, rire, rire, je vais mou"—it can be staged in all languages, in the same empty way, for no doubt the limits of my language are the limits of my world, but the limits of my world are also the limits of my lan-guage and, in the face of the death that is my anti-world, the impotence of my language becomes apparent.

Unpowerful language and powerless thinking certainly do not abandon the aging, not even when they despise the litany and aim to set up the dignity of their thinking human existence against death, that inevitable total defeat. They will then perhaps think of dying and more exactly dying away, the fear of which is justified, since physical torments of various degrees are ready for us. In fact, it is not unusual to say, "It's not death that I am afraid of, only sickness and pain." Who would try to contradict such hasty words? The torments of dying have been described many hundreds of times with gruesome urgency. One can read in Martin du Gard's *La Mort du Père*, "The crises of convulsive ure-mia grew more and more frequent; they unleashed themselves with such brutality that, after each one of these attacks, the nurses had to sit down breathless and watch the suffering of the sick man without doing anything. From one attack to another there was only a long howling, un long hurlement. . . ." One can find something similar in countless other passages. Many of us have also found ourselves present at death struggles similar to those that old Father Thibault battled with, where we've held someone's hands wet with sweat who writhed again and again in vain and was eventually buried, alas, the good soul. In order not to degenerate at this point into tedious chatter, and since doctors are already full of their gentle and optimistic solicitude, the aging who are in this situation stick to dying and put the unthinkable, death, out of mind. Provisionally. When they're not too easily exhausted and inclining to resignation, they will be compelled to find their way back to it. As they will learn later, this dying is also *living*, just as living is a permanent dying. "I know what death is," says Hofrat Behrens, speaking seriously for once and without his rhetorical high spirits, to the mother of the condemned Joachim Ziemssen in *The Magic Mountain*—"I am an old employee of his. Believe me, he's overrated. I can tell you, there's almost nothing to him. For whatever kinds of drudgery it may take beforehand in some cases, it's a frisky and lively affair and can lead to life and recovery. . . ."

It's this frisky and lively affair that first and foremost keeps the aging busy—so they think at least, before they climb down even deeper into the thought of death or the anti-thought of it. Furthermore, in a way vaguely comparable to concerns with order about life insurance and inheritance, this frisky and lively affair is partly a physical question and partly a social one. There's a big difference between the fear of dying of a heart attack, which at best throws one down in a few speedy minutes, and the fear of a uremic crisis that, like that of Père Thibault, draws on for weeks until his son, a doctor, no longer able to watch his father's suffering, gives the injection that delivers him. And it is not the same thing whether a poor devil dies in the hospital, alone, hardly noticed by indifferent nurses, or a rich man passes on in a luxury clinic: the flowers on his table, the well-honored, personally tinted care of the doctors, the visits of dependents that can happen every hour, may not really help him when it comes to that brief crossing over, but they do make those moments lighter that are free of torment. And then his good life is still present in his dying, the life that constantly distinguished his existence so drastically from the miserable life of the poor. We have to say it again and again: If we are all equal before death—which hardly means anything or, on the other hand, which only pushes the claim of equality back into the outrageous noncommitment of metaphysics—then we are still not equal before dying. "It is easier to cry with money," says an Eastern European Jewish dictum. It is also more comfortable to die with money; this and only this ought to be the meaning of Rilke's precious demand of God: he'd like to give everyone his or her own death. One's own or individual death can be purchased with money, just as one can purchase a personal life separated from the surging masses. And the social question of dying is just as unresolved as the nature of all social problems, even though there are those with their own interest who shamelessly make it appear to be already settled. Death, where is thy sting? The poor give a very precise answer: in the home for the aging, in the hospital, in the badly heated apartment where the mortally ill have to drag themselves through the corridor to the toilet.

One can no more hide and eventually conjure away the theme of social dying behind ontological considerations than the question about the more or less vehement bodily suffering, the torment, that precedes death. Yet on the other hand, it is impossible for us as thinking human beings to aim our explorations at *death* beyond the realities of dying without being fully conscious that our venture cannot be fulfilled, and we must make these explorations with strict discipline, avoiding the litany of an *idée fixe*. Yet we always get caught in the inconsistencies that, on the one hand, keep death and dying separate, and on the other, deny them again and again in a contradictory way; death is empty without dying, but the latter, too, has no contents without empty death. The gap that separates the vitality of dying from the total bleakness of death will open up first—and it is more than a platitude that a mortally ill person, groaning in pain, is something different from a silent cadaver. But already here—and with this we recognize the shady inexplicable relationship of death and dying—it becomes apparent that dying (not in the sense of the almost-nothing of crossing the threshold, but rather as dying away, grasped in its temporal structure) is a logically discussable concept. Certainly one can speak of dying without stepping beyond the field of everyday empiricism. Antoine Thibault, the young doctor who has established that the kidneys of his father are no longer filtering, knows that the old man lies there dying. But in a strict sense, since no one is dead before being dead, no one *dies* in the present. Again and again, it can only be said that one has *died*. Because it only gets its logical justification as a concept through the entrance of death, the word "die" is only applicable in logical language in forms of the past tense. That means nothing else than that human beings, in dealing with their end, are constantly coming again to death. But because death is unthinkable, all their efforts turn into nothing; its negativity puts all logical rules out of action. My death, an unreal question: as long as I am, it is not, and if it is, I am not any more. This we've known since antiquity, and such knowledge has never been any use to anyone for anything and is for everyone who approaches death only a tasteless joke. It is true. It is false. It is wisdom and folly. In fact, every subjective utterance about one's own death contains a logical problem. I am not. Doesn't this "I am" exclude the "not?" Not insofar as my utterance lets me both take myself out of myself and view my nonbeing or not-being-here as an objective fact, i.e., from the perspective of the survivor. Yes, the "I am" does not allow a "not" if I stay within myself and understand my ego as that which alone can have sense for me: as something being here.

The event of my death, the fact of my death, which in spite of all its logical problems concerns me more than all others and everything else, is only comprehensible for the survivors and only by them to be integrated into the course of affairs. A much told joke that is a bit of a horror story has a married man saying, "If one of the two of us dies, I will move into our country house." In French courts, the presiding judge rises, if a criminally accused person has died during the trial, and speaks the formula, "L'accusé est décédé, l'action publique est éteinte" (He is dead, the public action is dissolved). No more clearly and emphatically can one express the objective situation of the death of a human being who is now no more, against whom one can make no accusations, whom one cannot tax, nor pay, nor send to the front, and cannot put in a home for the aging. Except that, for a human being, his or her life is never a public matter no matter how much it is socially determined. That we are here and can no doubt think thoroughly of a world without our being here, not however our own not-being-here, is the fundamental matter of our existence. In certain moments it comes to be for us the meaning of the world plain and simple, even if it is an unbearable absurdity.

"I spit it out, for it is nothing for me," says the father Jaakob in Thomas Mann's Joseph tetralogy when he is brought the false report of Joseph's death. Thus everyone spits out the unheard-of impertinence that one should kindly come to terms with one's own death and one's own not being, for all human beings must eventually die. Each spits it out in the deepest disgust; no, it is nothing for him or her. All are all and one is oneself and when others die it is sad; that I, however, am not to be is a scandal and an impossibility. In a terrible, unnatural way, nevertheless, we human beings take what we've spit out again to ourselves. It is nothing for us, still we have to swallow it. We don't like to die and we will. We cannot think of death and we have to. The obviously unreal question, the exploration of the negative aspects of this frontier, the thinking of nothing that is at the same time a not-thinking—it is a person's last and most extreme question of being. "Le faux, c'est la mort" (falsehood is death), according to Jean-Paul Sartre. With that the philosopher renounces the death that makes existence an opaque essence, a stony *être* (being) that is still only an *avoir-été*, (a having-been). All those who get involved with death enter into more than a *liaison dangereuse*: they are committing an obscene incest. But one can also just as rightly say that the only thing that's true is death, since it is the future of all futures. Every step we take leads us to it, every thought we think breaks down on it. Its completely empty truth, its unreal reality is our life's meaningless fulfillment, our triumph over life only mastered in the nothingness of our border crossing, and our total debacle.

Death is the primal contradiction. As the absolute "not" it includes all other conceivable negations. It can only be negatively defined, the final decay of the last of all the billions of cells that make up our living organism. Negative thinking is not possible until we start with death, whose irreversibility first gives denial its totalizing meaning. That something was and no longer is: we only experience it through the death of others in the softened and veiled information brought to us by hospitals, funeral industries, and necropolises. A thing falls apart, but it can still be found again in another manifestation of being a thing. A human being, however, who has died, is gone, *parti sans laisser d'adresse* (departed without leaving a forwarding address) forever; by stiffening into a thing, a thing that as such decomposes just like every other thing, the human organism becomes its own denial. What happens with it after its death is only one more macabre, self-parodying, totally hopeless staging of an exhibition to cancel again the denial. The "dearly departed," "the loved one" about whose absurd post-mortem fate Evelyn Waugh reports in his like-named novel, is not just any dearly departed, but is *not*, and the ghastliness of that preparation by which a cadaver is treated with cosmetics and laid to rest among the cypresses—a rest that is no rest at all since the concept of rest presupposes that life's unrest will soon reappear—it is *mutatis mutandis* part and parcel of every celebratory interment.

Now, the experience of the death of others as the no-longer-being of something that was may well presuppose every negative and therefore dialectical kind of thinking. However, it is at the same time the rejection of all dialectic: the negation of a negation of a negation. Our disconsolate insight into not being is not a genuine insight but still one that lets us recognize from a distance a puzzling and fleeting shadow. It opens up a path to us for negative-dialectical thinking but closes it to us no sooner than we have entered upon it, for death is the negative that carries nothing positive within it. We understand an absolute negation, needed in order to use a relative negation, only from death, but in doing so we comprehend this negation itself no more than we comprehend death. Death as a contradiction, not only of every positive but also of all negative thinking—it is the nonsense that strikes back at every sense, it is mystery and triviality, necessity of thought and impossibility of thought, denial of life in a life that would be unimaginable and worthless without the boundary of death, but which at the same time loses every value since it has to end. Other than the physician determining a clinical death— these days no longer easy to define—or the public prosecutor who has to halt the public accusation of a person who has died, no one can talk about death without either talking contradictory nonsense or fleeing into metaphor. The metaphorical utterance, which we too cannot escape here, not even when we aspire to avoid it at all costs, is the more commodious and attractive way. The dead person rests or sleeps. "He's happy now," says the dependent of a man who has just died, in an anecdote by Alfred Polgar, and someone with a lot of nerve asks the coarse question, "How do you know?" The relative comforting himself and other family members with his assurance of well-being in death has no idea where he gets it from. The dead person—but what does that mean, the dead person? The nothing would have been a more correct way to say it, even if it is more empty, since the cadaver that will quickly decay is certainly not a "dead" thing. The dead person, if language usage wants it that way, is neither well nor unwell. It neither rests nor sleeps, for after rest, unrest must come and after sleep, awakening. "The not is not" would be the only, thoroughly tautological, way to assert it, and that we can drop.

Not only do the dead set the limits of their language with their death, but also those of ours over their being dead. *Requiescat in pace*—that is certainly a nice sounding phrase and quite rightly much more sympathetic to Hans Castorp than *Hoch soll er leben*,[1] which sounds more like raising the roof. But it is a metaphorically empty phrase, for no one rests in peace no matter how much we may wish it. Death does not wear a Spanish frill collar, nor is it the beautiful dark woman named Maria Casarès from Cocteau's *Orphée*, but it is empty and unrecognizable. No matter how often one starts to talk about death, it is false. "Not expressible in logical language." That's how Rudolf Carnap rules after semantic analysis of one of Heidegger's sentences about nothingness—and he's right. In metaphorical speech only babble is possible: thus any of us can pass judgment when we hear something about the eternal peace into which a person who has just died is supposed to be entering finally after a hard life—and every life is doubtless hard. To talk of the peace of death is nothing else than being horrified about the strife of life. But beyond that, the metaphors of death can no more be omitted than the correct utterance, made when someone has died, that only a negative that is not is there. Unless . . .

Yes, unless the metaphorically happy survivor, convinced that the dead person is happy now, believes in an eternal life and has defined this belief. This writer cannot relate to the absurdity of faith in a life that continues after death, a faith that only gains some sense through the medium of mythology. Right to the end, he remains entirely on the side of Jean Rostand, who said so simply and so emphatically, "I believe that when we fall it is forever and we don't get up again afterwards like the murdered actors in the theater."

All those who have banished the biomorphous and mythic hope for a continued existence beyond the boundary of death will not be able to abstain from the attempt, condemned to failure from the start, of thinking about their death. It is probably true, what Freud said, that particularly "in our unconscious everyone of us [is] convinced of his immortality"—and this, we would like to suggest, not so much from reasons of a creaturely clinging to life, but rather because one's own death is so unthinkable. On the other hand, our conviction is weak, just as shaky as the hope of living on held by those who call themselves believers in God. Père Thibault was a pious man, initiator and honorary chairman of numerous Catholic clubs. But when it got serious, then his God and the immortality in this God were clearly no longer worth much. He knows that the end is coming. "For the others death is a common, impersonal thought. For him it is now everything that is present, it is reality. He is death itself." And so he has his confessor come. The priest says what his *métier* calls for. Old Thibault is no longer within his reach. "For a moment, following the routine, his thinking tries to evoke the idea of God in order to flee to it. But his *élan* is immediately crippled. Eternal life, the grace of God—an unintelligible language: empty vocables lacking any common measure against the terrifying reality." No one believes in his or her death. Freud is right. When things come to a head, no one trusts the hope for a beyond: Martin du Gard, the writer of *The Thibaults*, is right.

At one time or another, everyone has to accept thinking the unthinkable. At one time or another. Of course, the point of time at which this empty exploration, the exploration of emptiness, begins is uncertain. Still, though conscious of saying something vague, one can speak of *aging* as the stretch of time in which we meet with the thought of death. For a young man—and we limit being young no more precisely than we specify the point at which a human being becomes aware of his aging—death is of no concern, even if he already has to bury close relatives. He goes to war, if not happily, at least without great fear of death; he hardly feels the dangerous speed of driving the car on the highway; even a serious illness usually does not cause him horror. "Wisdom of the body," confident of his ability to resist? That is only a question for biologists. Trust in global experience, gathering itself up as one statistic ahead of every other statistic, that young people have a longer life ahead of them than old people? Please find an answer from psychology. What the aging think they know is twofold: that on the one hand the fear of death or the urgency of the thought of death have different grades according to whether one expects death from outside—by accident or from the hand of an enemy—or death from within; that on the other hand even this death of a young person from within, even if he or she is heavily suffering, has only a slight value in reality. It requires an extensive experience of physical downfall, dwindling bodily powers, weakened memory, decay, and difficulty in all forms, for death to change from an objectively impersonal subject into something authentic. It may only be a logically untenable analogy and metaphor to say things like, "We live in a long process of dying," "We die without cease," "Death grows up inside of us"—in the region of lived experience such metaphoric characterizations of death are experienced reality. As long as the aging do not pursue the business of suppressing this awareness without a bad conscience and with only a little success, if they do not alienate themselves with some kind of operational fitness for living, they sense that they are dying many years before they actually pass away. Their physical, social, and cultural loss of the world makes them certain of something they had only believed earlier and without feeling to be a theoretical truth: that they are *moribundi*. The temptation to recite a manic litany appears to them. I will die, I will die, die, die. They are now dependent on death, on something that does not form any part of their possibilities. But since they very quickly recognize that besides a lyrical death-stammer there is nothing anyone can do with an annihilating nothingness, they arrive again and again at the horrible frisky vitality of dying.

Nothing will be taken back: the verb die can only be used logically in the past tense since it does not receive its legitimization until death has already taken place. Still, since the contradiction of death overshadowing our entire life makes all logic—which is surely always the logic of life—and all positive thinking invalid, ideas of death have to take their shape in opposition to logic in thoughts of dying. The afflicted may then say to themselves, they have to think around death, since they cannot think about death—and constantly try this roundabout way anew even though they constantly describe only half-circles. I will die, say the aging to themselves. When? Where? How? Above all: how?

A few years ago it was A.'s turn: birthdays with unbelievably high figures and bodily inconveniences of all kinds no longer permitted him to live for the day like a nice brute or his plucky neighbor. He was supposed to be familiar with death—not with that of the others, like the chief physician Privy Councilor Behrens who in the Berghof Sanatorium is death's old employee, but with his own. A. had lived for years under definite, though here not pertinent, circumstances in which every day and every hour he had to expect his death. He had seen those like him depart in just about every conceivable way. His comrades (it can't be expressed otherwise) had *croaked*, as it turned out exactly, from typhus, dysentery, hunger, from the blows with which they were tortured, even snapping for breath in Zyklon B. He had carelessly climbed over piles of bodies, stridden through underground corridors in which some had been strung up on powerful iron hooks. How was it with me at that time, A. asks himself and gives himself an answer, knowing that others will accept it with distrust: I was not afraid. I was not brave, because there was a lot that terrified me. I was young. And the death that threatened me came from outside: there is no nicer death in the world than being killed by an enemy. It came from outside, even when it was not the death of a cudgel or gas. Dysentery and phlegmon were attacks by an enemy world, terrifying as such but not causing fear like that slow dying, assigned to me in my decay from within as a familiar enemy with whom I have to deal, now that I have aged and have been made to understand by not exactly pleasant diagnoses of physicians and a few numerical figures that I am going downhill. Dying by *murder*, which in my case could even have been conceived at that time as a death from within, is an attack of the world against my person. A steel pipe strikes, a shot is fired, a sudden fever throws me down. I stand then—stood, as I precisely remember—in the condition of a human being who has lost his trust in the world because in his distress he cannot cherish any expectation of help. Dying was terror.

Now it is *horror* and *angor*, horror and anguish. I had to expect quite literally that a boot would kick me to pieces or half kick me to pieces and no one would even give my mashed body as much as a glance, let alone bring it active assistance. Such fright has something precipitous, incomprehensible, something thoroughly alien about it, but even if I was unarmed, there had still persisted an irrational basic state of affairs in which a germ of a possible defense lay embedded.

Today? I deny myself nothing. On account of a trifle I go to the doctor. He is friendly, his instruments and his prescription pad are there to serve me. I dragged around for days at twenty degrees below zero Celsius and across I don't know how many kilometers of snow-covered highways, and every now and then I heard the whip-snap of a shot that brought a comrade down. The strange fright made me perhaps tremble a short time perhaps, but I was spared from fear.

When I am tired and do not want to drive my own car, I take a taxi; it's all rather comfortable, and no one denies good service to anyone who can lay out a few pieces of money. But fear is with me, a deaf feeling that never makes me tremble, just an extremely persistent one, which in a slow kind of way becomes a part of my person, so much so that I cannot actually say any longer that I *have* any fear. Instead I say that I *am* fear, even though this sense of being fear does not hinder me in doing my work, even though others know nothing of it, and even the good mood I wear for appearance hardly suffers any damage. I cherish the strong suspicion that it is no better with other aging people who, if need be, organize happy picnics, go to the theater, and have fashionable clothing made for themselves. As for me, a man of the long death march of a former age who is not any braver but also not especially faint-hearted, I know in any case that I become afraid of dying to the degree that the hopes of life abandon me. The ontic density of my existence gets thin and the fear of dying fills up the empty space as pure negativity. The slow advance of what will eventually be my death has given my life its particular, very ugly, and to me previously unknown color. I do not know exactly anymore how it happened when I first began to perceive the step, the hoof beat, and trot. Getting tired too quickly in one place, heavy breathing, a startling pain in another; even without being able to remember it, it becomes reality in retrospect. Not until all sorts of injury had already grown stronger were aging and expectation of death present as constituting elements. Fear, *angor, angustiae,* constriction, anguish. I often think about the snow-covered highways of 1944 and the good death by murder that didn't want to know me at all. No nicer death, as a matter of fact—not everyone has the chance.

An unacceptable thought when one considers the reactionary vulgarities for which it could provide an alibi! And what folly to wish for a death that's already happened out of fear of dying! But it is only the folly of death's contradiction, which extinguishes every reflective thought. It remains true, I am certain, that, if no time was passing, it was easier to die and easier to become intimate with something so unavoidable and unthinkable. Or if it didn't get that far, the event, inevitably approaching and inconceivable in its specificity, could be in the course of the inexorable aging process— how does one complete this predicate? It won't work with "perceived in advance," since we're dealing with something completely unknown. Can everything eventually be reduced to the word "feared?" I am frightened of dying, against which I argued in familiar hostility while aging and to which I became accustomed in deceptive intimacy. I don't know it—how could any living person know it? —and therefore have to tie it to experiences of life, if I am to say anything more than repetitious talk about anxiety and "fear," knowing by the way that this more for which I yearn can only be a pretext. I think I am afraid of constriction. It's probably not very much out of line to put dying on the same level as the constriction of my life. The body interferes just the same. To be abandoned by life, to take the last breath, "to sigh away," as it is called in a passage very dear to me, means suffocating as I understand it, even if medical science dismisses this concept as clinically imprecise. For with breathing, which will then be denied to me, I am just as familiar as everyone else. I have had shortness of breath as much as anyone: that made it clear to me that the wish for freedom can be taken back to the impulsive desire for freedom to breathe. But in dying the amount of oxygen I so thoroughly want for myself is no longer granted me. With the freedom to breathe denied, all freedoms withdraw themselves from me. Anxious for air I have to go on—that is the basest thing—with a fear that with great likelihood I'll get to know more and more precisely.

For A., who thinks he knows something about death and dying, the presence of death in life is the slow withering away that comes to be known with aging; and this he again ascribes to fear of constriction and suffocation. He thinks there is something peculiar about this shortness of breath. It turns every reflection into the absurdity of the anti-thought of death, as is obvious to anyone longing hopelessly to escape from threatening constrictions. One does not have to be a physician and a patient to know that shortness of breath makes anyone oppressed in this way want to breathe even more deeply instead of yearning for the dupery of a salvation through death. This salvation does not exist. A suffering person can always be released from his or her torment into a life free of torment, into the gratification of an ego free of distress, but never *from* this ego. Only when a person no longer *has* pain but in physical and psychic totality *is* pain, as in the case of a carcinoma with bone metastases, may the absurd desire for negation, for the anti-ego of nothingness, appear. But even in this most extreme torture, inflicted on the sick by their own bodies, the suffering individuals will still desire to breathe, even if they have implored their physician to make an end to their misery with an injection.

Therefore, in spite of all logical contradiction, it seems that the fear of dying, made concrete in the shortness of breath, is in the end still the fear of death. While thinking of dying we cannot stick to the vitality of the final event but are always directed to the thought of death in its impossibility, partly because it is only from death that dying actually becomes dying, partly however—and here A.'s, or anyone's, experience of shortness of breath helps us further—because no suffering person ever accepts a single breath as the last, "delivering" one. The fear of dying or of suffocating accordingly becomes the horror of death, which, on authority of ancient wisdom, is no concern of ours. And now the next step in this inquiry into the unknowable can be taken easily, all too easily perhaps, making it better to approach as a question rather than an answer that sounds insolent. Can't we conclude that not only the fear of dying but every fear actually goes back to the fear of death? Not to deduct anything from the vindicated legitimacy of A.'s brooding distinction between terror on the one hand, horror and anguish on the other, between the death that is inflicted upon us from without, as something foreign, and the difficult one which—to speak metaphorically—grows on us from within in the most evil of all intimacies. It is certain, however, that in our sighing away horror and terror combine again as the fear of death—and the question about reducing every fear to the fear of suffocation or death may be asked but not precisely answered. When we go to the doctor, we calm down when he or she diagnoses the pains that we endure as harmless. Oppressive and thoroughly painful rheumatoid sufferings, which one knows will not lead to death, can be absorbed by the person of the patient better than initially painless but life-threatening illnesses of the circulation or the blood. In his incomparably thoughtful book, *Wohlbefinden und Mißbefinden* (Feeling well and feeling sick), the German physician and phenomenologist Herbert Plügge tells us about a so-called dynamic forty-five-year-old industrialist who goes to him with what he, the patient, believes to be rheumatoid pains in his left shoulder and briskly excuses himself in the process for troubling a professor of medicine with such a trifle. When the examination reveals that it is in no way a question of rheumatism but of clear symptoms of *angina pectoris* and the physician lets the patient know his diagnosis, a remarkable change takes place in the man. Even though he certainly does not suffer physically any more than before, his vigor and dynamism are all gone. "Fourteen days later he acted as though he had grown old," writes Herbert Plügge. "His manner was inhibited, his elasticity gone. He now lives fastidiously, has given up smoking, has himself driven by a chauffeur. He 'notices' his heart now and is depressed." He is, one may well add, afraid, afraid of dying, afraid of death, afraid to hold his breath in fear that it may be his last. "L'angoisse diffuse, l'angoisse ultime, enfin, s'appelle la mort" (All-pervasive fear, the final fear—in short—is called death), writes Vladimir Jankélévitch. Every fear is fear of death, every care is to keep us from death; what we "do for our health" is directed defensively against death. Our entire life passes away in the absurd effort to avoid the unavoidable: the more we "die" and the closer we come to our last breath, the more desperately we struggle against something with which, in order to be sensible, it is our business to reconcile ourselves. Sensible? We find ourselves in a place where it is all over with every form of being sensible, where we're dealing with death, which is absolute non-sense. To reconcile ourselves: that means to accept death. But that would mean refusing life on the spot. Neither the one nor the other is possible. Every refusal has to guarantee us even the most miserable alternative. Death in its total alien and incomprehensible nature is no alternative. It is the false, since we cannot think it, and the true, since it is fully certain for us. Before the opacity of the No that is set against us and given to us, we come to be nothing even before we come not to be.

How do we conduct ourselves? Do we murmur a monomaniac litany? Do we make our peace with the negativity encompassing us? Do we flee from death into death? Do we continue to live on as if we weren't already promised to death?

When it comes to individual psychology, answers to such questions will always vary from one person to the next. We know examples of "carefree" individuals who live on into aging and old age without a care. They live in equilibrium, so it seems in any case and so they assure us; dying and death do not concern them at all. There are others—we call them disturbed—who, in running away from death, run to death and imagine, God knows, that the act that seals their loss of freedom beyond recall, suicide, is the confirmation of their freedom. If mental derangement hadn't beaten him to it, Nietzsche might have acted this way, since he wrote, "Death is only a death that is not free under despised conditions, a death at the wrong time, a cowardly death. Out of love for life one ought to want death differently, free, conscious, without surprise." A fool's story of a voluntary death.

We hear of the brave who peacefully look death in the eye (as if there was one, as if there was anything at all to see there) and die upright in opposition to the geotropism, the gravitation of aging that pulls them earthward. There are reports of cheerful types who approach their end in serenity, of those who are agitated in panic and raise up a clamor as soon as the first harbinger of the end comes to them and who never stop howling so that even those who love them turn away from them, their hearts full of impatience, and heave a sigh of relief when finally death releases, not the one who is wailing, but them. Beyond every individual particularity, however, there is perhaps still—and with this the realm of psychology is abandoned—a fundamentally similar form of conduct in the face of death and dying, conditioned by the similarity of our fundamental destiny, in which the brave and the cowardly, the robust and the sickly, the cheerfully at peace with themselves and the disturbed neurotics find each other in full equality. In aging, they all make a compromise with death. Not peace, just a compromise, a bad compromise, no matter how unpleasant that might sound. In doing so, it's not as if they've learned how to die. It isn't learned in familiarity. It comes about right when one realizes that it can't be learned, when one's "advanced sensing" is reduced to fear, in the unendurable feeling of constriction, in the absolute horror of the last breath. The bad compromise is a precariously standing, but from case to case more or less deeply disturbed, but never, even to the neurotic hypochondriac, entirely lacking balance of fear and confidence, rebellion and resignation, refusal and acceptance. The aging, for whom dying changes from a universal and objective matter to a personal one, try to neutralize the proximity of the Big Moment, a nearness that is clearly evident in statistics and medical findings, by means of a confidence that is not confident in itself and that every day becomes more irrational. Every deferment—after a seizure, a serious illness, a dangerous operation—is for them like an appeal to a law court that can actually acquit them. Illusion: for here matters are really delayed, not suspended, and the judges do not think at all of cassation. But that does not hinder the aging from being taken in by the hallucination they know to be just that. In Finnish, there is apparently an evening prayer in which it is said, "Lord, I gladly want to follow you if you call me, but not in this night." Those who know they're getting closer to death act as if they're in an unstable equilibrium, like people praying. They already want to die (they don't, they just know that they have to and therefore say they're getting ready)—but not tonight, just not at this hour.

Every night is tonight and every hour is this hour, and every time an appeal is made to the court.

To live with dying is not intended to mean that we grasp the knowledge of our own finitude. It also doesn't mean that we habituate ourselves to the nonsense of nothingness. Habituation is only a certain exercise in empty and false expectation, in the self-deception of being a victim by *not* being that victim since one eventually knows that at some time, and probably very soon, the judgment will become legally binding and be executed.

The astonishing capability of the aging to adapt themselves to a feeling for time appropriately required by the circumstances makes it easy for them to establish a balance. As we said at another point, they become time more and more in memory, for world and space withdraw from them. We also said of time-in-the-future that it should not be discussed; death, denial of every contingency, is the goal of expectation and cancels the sense of the concept of the future. We are not giving up on this position. Yet it seems necessary to replace it with something new and different, even if we are not going to introduce again the dimension of the future that has become senseless for the aging. Future, whatever is coming to us, we said, is space in the reality of the lived; the aging lose the former with the latter. What they exchange for it is a feeling of indistinct and definitely sloppy temporal indifference. It does not exclude their fear, but on the contrary includes it and makes it even bearable. They look back into a past of moving backgrounds of years and stages of life that change their quantitative value in the process of remembering. But it is always the case that every arbitrary time span from the past seems tiny to them, while they cannot even foresee the same stretch of time in a shadowy and dubious future. Precisely because they have to reckon with the possibility of being alive for only a few more years, they likewise let the Good Lord be a good man who will certainly extend the span into infinity. Four years ago one of them was in some old city on vacation: that was yesterday. In one year he will no longer be here: but how long does a year last! The disintegrating extension of a posterior period of time, ontically losing its density, belongs to the process of balance and accommodation just as the illusory appeal to the court. With this concept we would give ourselves away to theology, to any sort of transcendental thinking which, as Gabriel Marcel expresses it, looks at "hope" as the stuff "of which our soul is made." Let's avoid that kind of guilelessness. When the aging make their bad compromise, they act as creatures of fear who have to stand up in that fear and against it.

Creatures of negation, containing no kind of positivity that can be described dialectically, they evade with a bad conscience a No that constantly takes hold of them again. They play hide and seek with death even when they try to deal with it. Père Thibault, tormented by the pain of his uremic attack, receives an injection from his son. "He feels a kind of release of tension," writes his inventor, Roger Martin du Gard, "a need for rest that was exquisite because there was no fatigue along with it. He had not stopped thinking of his death, but now, since he had stopped believing in death under the effects of the injection, it became possible for him, even agreeable, to speak about it." All aging persons, even when feeling healthy and robust, are a Père Thibault, accepting his death as an objective event whenever it doesn't threaten him directly and saying to himself, "Naturally, I will die but it will still take a good while for that"—which means the same thing as a vast, unimaginably long time. He goes into convulsions, without hope, whenever he really thinks he is standing at the frontier and death in its negativity is the only authentic thing remaining to him. "Just a little minute longer, Mr. Executioner," implored the Countess Dubarry on the scaffold. Her request has the same meaning as the Finnish prayer. It is an expression of the same tragic error, that postponement means cancellation and that the next moment couldn't just as easily, in the same radical and irrevocable way, be, like this one, her last. The tiny stretch of time from one moment to the next, when only another respite is granted, has the same messy infinity as the year or the decade that human beings still hope for themselves.

The aging live on in a false compromise with the inability of escaping their condition, realized at whatever occasion they first felt themselves to be aging. But in telling themselves these tall stories of their compromise, they are not despicable liars, and their *mauvaise foi* is not that of common swindlers. To be sure, the untruth with which they comply, the bad compromise into which they enter, is only the psychic counterpart of just this constitution, forced from the absurdity of their fundamental condition: the more profoundly the false, or perhaps better: the more that which falsifies—death—overshadows them, the falser their life will be. The closer the No gets to them, the more distorted and insincere their Yes becomes. Whenever the ring of constriction, of anguish, closes around them, pressing harder and harder, something compels them, ever more hopelessly and therefore more desperately and dishonestly, toward explosion and distance. They say to the moment: "Stay!"—and know that it's not beautiful and that it won't come to a stop with them. They play many different roles—the brave ones, the quietly surrendering, the stirred up in panic, the proud rebels—and they can't make any of their interpretations believable, since they are registered in all texts as unbelievable and unplayable. They think about death and dying, pulling them apart and then putting them back together again, they separate the alien death by murder from their intimate enemy, slowly accruing to them, they brood over their fear and the time period accorded to their deceptive solace. It is all in vain. The absurdity of death negates whatever they think up for themselves but urges them on with their thinking. The cares they consider are the unclear mirror image of their cares of death, since no one can lead a life with the former and suppress the latter. One aging man thinks of his grippe, of his debts, of his unfaithful lover. And he's not to think of death, even if the grippe is still curable, the debt payable, the faithless woman replaceable, while with death, which ends everything, nothing can be done? A. is up to his neck, up to his mouth, in thoughts of death, which won't reflect much literary credit on him. One should leave him alone. He is an A., an aging human being; credit doesn't matter to him.

"Whoever does not want to die young, has to die old," that is one of those platitudes in which nonsense, profundity, and clarity are all in agreement. No one wants to die young, no one wants to get old: there we have the complementary banality that only heightens what is supplemented by the unfathomable dimension of the unacceptable aspects of a self-consuming existence that we always accept. Aging, through which the Not and the "un" of our existence make themselves known and become evident to us, is a desolate region of life, lacking any reasonable consolation; one should not fool oneself. In aging we become the worldless inner sense of pure time. As aging people we become alien to our bodies and at the same time closer to their sluggish mass than ever before. When we have passed beyond the prime of life, society forbids us to continue to project ourselves into the future, and culture becomes a burdensome culture that we no longer understand, that instead gives us to understand that, as scrap iron of the mind, we belong to the waste heaps of the epoch. In aging, finally, we have to live with dying, a scandalous imposition, a humiliation without compare, that we put up with, not in humility, but as the humiliated. All symptoms of the incurable sickness can be taken back to the incomprehensible effects of the death-virus we have when we enter the world. It was not virulent when we were young. We certainly knew of it, but it didn't matter to us. With aging, it comes out of its latency. It is our affair, our only one, even when it is nothing, and the manic litany, the poetic prattle of death, is still better than the fundamentally ugly kitsch of the idyllic evening sun. "Old age should burn and rave at close of day," says Dylan Thomas.

Has A. done something to disturb the balance, expose the compromise, destroy the genre painting, contaminate the consolation? He hopes so. The days shrink and dry up. He has the desire to tell the truth.

# NOTES

## TRANSLATOR'S INTRODUCTION

1. *A Leopardi Reader*, ed. and trans. Ottavio M. Casale (Urbana: University of Illinois Press, 1981), p. 215. The comment from the *Pensieri* occurs on p. 189.

2. *At the Mind's Limits: Contemplations by a Survivor on Auschwitz and Its Realities*, trans. Sidney Rosenfeld and Stella P. Rosenfeld, with an afterword by Sidney Rosenfeld and a foreword by Alexander Stille (New York: Schocken Books, 1990), p. 20.

3. *Der integrale Humanismus: Aufsätze und Kritiken eines Lesers, 1966–1978*, ed. with an afterword by Helmut Heissenbüttel (Stuttgart: Klett-Cotta, 1985), pp. 219, 221.

4. *Radical Humanism: Selected Essays*, ed. and trans. Sidney Rosenfeld and Stella P. Rosenfeld (Bloomington: Indiana University Press, 1984), p. 3.

5. *Jenseits von Schuld und Sühne: Bewältigungsversuche eines Überwältigten* (Munich: Szczesny, 1966); first published in English as *At the Mind's Limits* in the translation of Sidney Rosenfeld and Stella P. Rosenfeld by Indiana University Press in 1980.

6. *Radical Humanism*, p. 5.

7. *Charles Bovary, Landarzt: Porträt eines einfachen Mannes* (Stuttgart: Klett-Cotta, 1978).

8. *Hand an sich legen: Diskurs über den Freitod* (Stuttgart: Klett, 1976).

9. *Text + Kritik 99: Jean Améry* (July 1988), p. 67.

10. "Jean Améry's essay *Über das Altern*: Ein Dialog mit französischen Dichtern und Denkern," in *Über Jean Améry*, ed. Irene Heidelberger-Leonard (Heidelberg: Carl Winter, 1990), pp. 79–90.

11. *Text + Kritik 99*, p. 69.

## PREFACE TO THE FOURTH EDITION

1. Allusion to the play *Der Verschwender* (The spendthrift) by Ferdinand Raimund (1790–1836).

PREFACE TO THE FIRST EDITION

1. Vladimir Jankélévitch: *La mort* (Paris, 1967). Herbert Plügge: *Wohlbefinden und Mißbefinden* (Tübingen, 1962); *Der Mensch und sein Leib* (Tübingen, 1967). André Gorz: *Le vieillissement*, in *Les Temps Modernes*, nos. 187 and 188. [Améry's note]

EXISTENCE AND THE PASSAGE OF TIME

1. Allusion to the poem "Tristan," by August von Platen (1796–1835).
2. Allusion to *Faust*, by Johann Wolfgang von Goethe (1749–1832): according to his pact with Mephistopheles, Faust would forfeit his soul if he ever became satisfied and asked time to stop for a moment, saying, "Verweile doch, du bist so schön" (Tarry a while, you are so lovely).
3. The first line of a poem by Walther von der Vogelweide (c. 1170–1230), written late in his life.
4. Allusion to the opening of *Joseph and His Brothers* by Thomas Mann (1875–1955).
5. Eugène Ionesco, *Exit the King* in *Plays*, vol. 4, trans. Donald Watson (London: John Calder, 1963), p. 35.
6. Allusion to the poem "Hyperions Schicksalslied" (Hyperion's song of destiny) by Friedrich Hölderlin (1770–1843).
7. Monk of Heisterbach: Caesarius von Heisterbach (c.1180–1240), a monk who wrote moral tales.

STRANGER TO ONESELF

1. This quotation and the two that follow, from Simone de Beauvoir, *Force of Circumstance*, trans. Richard Howard (New York: Putnam, 1965), p. 656.
2. Apparently Herbert Plügge.
3. Signor Settembrini and "life's young problem child" (Hans Castorp): characters in Thomas Mann's novel *The Magic Mountain*.

THE LOOK OF OTHERS

1. Allusion to the title of a chapter in *The Magic Mountain* about the death of Hans Castorp's cousin, a soldier.

2. Theodor Fontane: German novelist (1819–1898), all of whose novels were written after he turned fifty-nine.

3. The first line of a poem "Verborgenheit" (Seclusion), by Eduard Mörike (1804–1875).

NOT TO UNDERSTAND THE WORLD ANYMORE

1. Lettrism: a literary movement that tried to find poetry in the letters of the alphabet by emphasizing graphic sequences, often without apparent meaning.

2. Witch's one-times-one (Hexeneinmaleins): Goethe's *Faust*, line 2,552, where the witch in the scene "Witch's Kitchen" declaims nonsense verse about the magic use of numbers.

3. Theodor Lessing (1872–1933) and Ludwig Klages (1872–1956): German thinkers well known in the German-speaking world in the 1920s.

4. The German word here is *hold*, meaning "lovely" and "sweet." The English word "comely," with its combination of poetic, archaic, and morally proper connotations comes as close as possible to *hold*, which contains all those connotations with perhaps greater intensity.

5. Christian Sinding (1856–1941): Norwegian composer. Detlev von Liliencron (1844–1909) and Theodor Storm (1817–1888) were poets widely read in the German-speaking world during the early years of the twentieth century. After 1800, Hölderlin's poetry underwent a dramatic transformation that has defined his modern reputation.

6. Allusions to Hölderlin's poem "Hälfte des Lebens" (Half of life) and the use of an imaginary language by the poet Richard Dehmel (1863–1920).

7. Andreas Gryphius (1616–1664): German poet and dramatist.

8. Cf. Goethe's "Selige Sehnsucht" (Blessed yearning).

9. Allusion (also in the title of this chapter) to the final words of the play *Maria Magdalene* by Friedrich Hebbel (1813–1863).

TO LIVE WITH DYING

1. "Hoch soll er leben" is a German equivalent of "For he's a jolly good fellow," but it contains in it the suggestion that one should live to a ripe old age (*ein hohes Alter*) and is therefore actually less of a "metaphorically empty" phrase than "Requiescat in pace" (Rest in peace).

Jean Améry was born in Vienna in 1911 as Hanns Mayer. As a young man, he studied philosophy and wanted to be a novelist. When the Nazis came to power in Austria in 1938, he fled to Belgium and joined the resistance there. He was caught distributing leaflets, tortured, and sent to Auschwitz. He survived, and after the war he made his home in Brussels, changing his name to Jean Améry. In 1966, he published *Jenseits von Schuld und Sühne* (*At the Mind's Limits*), a series of essays about his experiences in Auschwitz, which made him famous.

John D. Barlow is Dean of the School of Liberal Arts at Indiana University-Purdue University at Indianapolis. He is a professor of English and German and author of *German Expressionist Film.*